The Russian Army of 1696-1796
From Peter the Great to Catherine the Great

By
Gabriele Esposito

The Russian Army of 1696 - 1796 by Gabriele Esposito
Cover image by Richard Knotel

This edition published in 2024

Winged Hussar Publishing is an imprint of

Winged Hussar Publishing, LLC
1525 Hulse Rd, Unit 1
Point Pleasant, NJ 08742

Copyright © Winged Hussar Publishing
ISBN PB 978-1-950423-97-2

LCN 2024941562

Bibliographical References and Index
1. History. 2. Russia. 3. 18th Century

Winged Hussar Publishing, LLC All rights reserved
For more information
visit us at www.whpsupplyroom.com

Twitter: WingHusPubLLC
Facebook: Winged Hussar Publishing LLC

This book is sold subject to the condition that it shall not, by way of trade or otherwise, be lent, resold, hired out, or otherwise circulated without the publisher's prior consent in any form of binding or cover other than that in which it is published and without a similar condition, including this condition, being imposed on the subsequent purchaser.

The scanning, uploading, and distribution of this book via the Internet or via any other means without the permission of the publisher is illegal and punishable by law. Please purchase only authorized electronic editions, and do not participate in or encourage electronic piracy of copyrighted materials. Your support of the author's and publisher's rights is appreciated. Karma, it's everywhere.

About the author

Gabriele Esposito is a military historian who works as a freelance author and researcher for some of the most important publishing houses in the military history sector. In particular, he is an expert specializing on uniformology: his interests and expertise range from the ancient civilizations to modern post-colonial conflicts. During recent years he has conducted and published several works on the military history of the Latin American countries, with special attention on the War of the Triple Alliance and the War of the Pacific. He is among the leading experts on the military history of the Italian Wars of Unification and the Spanish Carlist Wars. His books and essays are published on a regular basis by Osprey Publishing, Pen & Sword, Winged Hussar Publishing and Libreria Editrice Goriziana; he is also the author of numerous military history articles appearing in specialized magazines like *Ancient Warfare Magazine*, *Medieval Warfare Magazine*, *The Armourer*, *History of War*, *Guerres et Histoire*, *Focus Storia* and *Focus Storia Wars*.

Acknowledgements

The written text of the present book contains a lot of info that has never been published before in English, which has been obtained from a series of important sources written in different languages (Russian, Ukrainian and Polish). It would have been impossible for the author to translate these sources in English without the decisive help of some precious friends who are well-known experts of military history: Vincent Rospond for the Russian sources, Serge Shamenkov and Oleksii Sokyrko for the Ukrainian sources, Jacek Jaworski for the Polish sources. The present work is illustrated with many plates taken from Aleksandr Vasilevich Viskovatov's massive books on the evolution of Russian military uniforms across time. Viskovatov's publications, the most important and respected authority on Russian uniformology, were published during the central decades of the 19th century and thus are in the public domain since long time. They are an incredible free source of materials for any researcher interested in the history of the Russian military institutions. The plates by Viskovatov that are reproduced in this book are taken from the colourized version of his famous work, which was published in a luxury edition during 1841-1862. All Viskovatov's volumes of this edition are available in digital format and can be freely downloaded from the excellent Runivers.ru website.

Table of Contents

Russia and Eastern Europe in the Early 18th Century 2

The Russian Army of Peter the Great 7

The Russian Army of Empress Anna, 1730 - 1740 19

The Russian Army of Empress Elizabeth, 1741 - 1762 30

The Holstein Army of Peter III, 1762 44

The Russian Army of Catherine the Great, 1762 - 1796 ... 52

The Grant Hetmanate of Ukraine 99

Russian Regimental Flags and Colors 105

Bibliography 110

Russia and Eastern Europe in the early 18th century

The main aim of the present book is to present a detailed overview of the history, organization and uniforms of the Russian Army during the 18th century from the ascendancy of Peter the Great in 1696 to the death of Catherine the Great in 1796. The general evolution of the Russian military forces will be covered from the beginning to the end of the 18th century, explaining how Tsar Peter the Great built up the modern Russian Army during the Great Northern War (1700-1721) and how this was progressively enlarged until being involved into the French Revolutionary Wars since 1798. All the branches of service of the Russian Army will be covered with full detail: Imperial Guard, line infantry, light infantry, heavy cavalry, medium cavalry, light cavalry, Cossacks, irregular cavalry, artillery, engineers, garrison troops, foreign corps and naval troops. Catherine the Great (ruling during 1762-1796) is considered by many historians as one of the great monarchs in the history of Russia, since she was able to transform her country into a first-rate military power by conquering large portions of Eastern Europe and Asia. During her reign, Empress Catherine fought several wars: the "War of the Bar Confederation" (1768-1772) against the aristocracy of Poland-Lithuania, the "First Turkish War" (1768-1774) against the Ottoman Empire, the "Second Turkish War" (1787-1792) against the Ottoman Empire, the "Swedish War" (1788-1790) against Sweden, the "First Polish War" (1792) against the Polish-Lithuanian Commonwealth and the "Second Polish War" (1792) against the Polish-Lithuanian patriots. These bloody conflicts led to the Russian conquest of large areas of Poland, Lithuania, Belarus, Ukraine, the Crimea and Caucasus. For this reason, we have decided to provide an overview of the military forces that fought more frequently against the Russian Army during the second half of the 18th century. These were the Polish-Lithuanian Army and the Zaporizhian Army of Ukraine, which were both partly absorbed by the Russian military forces after having been defeated by the latter.

The modern Russian state emerged as a first-rate European military power only after the dramatic events of the Great Northern War (1700-1721). This conflict was one of the largest and most important wars ever fought in the Baltic region: it saw the heavy involvement of all the states located in northern and eastern Europe, lasting for two decades. At the beginning of the 18th century, after the many wars that had followed the Peace of Westphalia of 1648, the political landscape in Europe was in flux: occurring more or less during the same years of the Great Northern War, in fact, the countries of central and southern Europe were ravaged by the long and terrible War of the Spanish Succession. Both these conflicts had enduring consequences for the future history of the states that fought them. In regard to the Great Northern War, it is important to note that it marked the promotion of Russia as a real "great power" of Europe: until the ascendancy of Peter the Great, in fact, she had remained mired in the political scene of eastern Europe. The hard lessons learned during the Great Northern War and the consequent "westernization" of the state realized by Peter the Great transformed Russia into the dominant military power of the Baltic area and into a major player in western politics.

In 1700, when the conflict began, Sweden was one of the European "great powers" and controlled most of northern Europe: thanks to the great military victories of Gustavus Adolphus during the Thirty Years' War, in fact, the Scandinavian country had created a real "empire" that comprised large and rich territories. In addition to Finland, which was traditionally a dominion of the Swedish Crown, the Swedish Empire

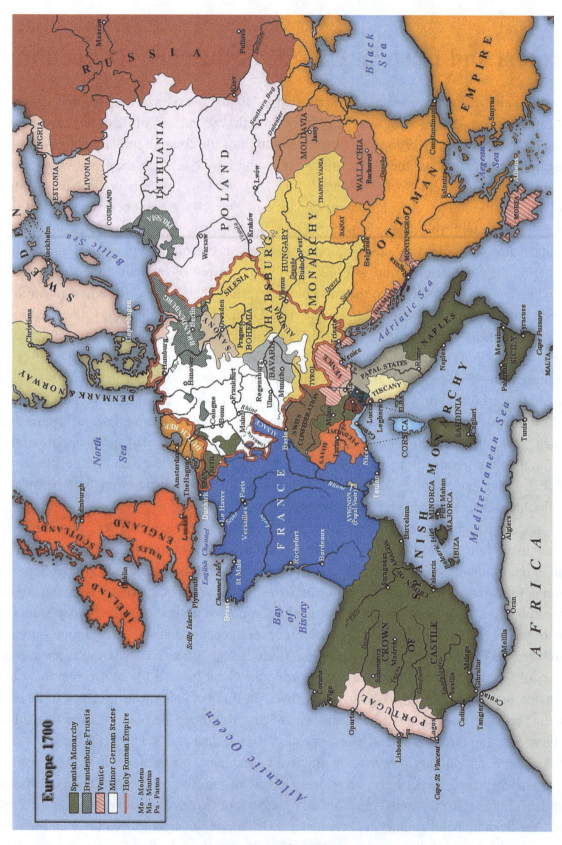

Europe in 1700

included the following territories: Karelia (a border region located between Finland and Russia), Ingria (the coastal region of Russia on the Baltic, where Saint Petersburg was later founded), Estonia, Livonia (more or less corresponding to modern Latvia) and several areas on the northern coast of Germany (Western Pomerania, Wismar, Duchy of Bremen and Verden). The large dimensions of the Swedish possessions meant that they had to be defended from several enemies: after many decades of successes, with the beginning of the new century, the Swedes had to face the new Russian menace and a large coalition of old enemies. The latter had contrasting ambitions but shared one important objective: the destruction of the Swedish Empire, in order to expand their areas of influence over former Swedish territories.

Russia and Sweden were the major participants to the Great Northern War, two great military powers that were able to deploy several armies on many different fronts; it is important to remember, however, that the Great Northern War was a large conflict involving many different states. The military coalition guided by Russia included many old enemies of Sweden, first of these was the Kingdom of Denmark-Norway. Frederick IV of Denmark had great ambitions for his country, especially regarding dominance over Scandinavia for control of the Baltic commerce. From the secession of Sweden from the Kalmar Union in 1523, Denmark had always tried to maintain its leadership position among the Scandinavian countries. After the Thirty Years' War, however, Sweden had been able to build up an empire and to reduce the international influence of Denmark. After 1648 Sweden and Denmark had fought each other during 1657-1660 and in the Scanian War of 1675-1679; the latter conflict was extremely harsh for both sides but led to no significant political or territorial changes. Many questions remained unsettled between Sweden and Denmark, with the result that in 1700 the Danes were ready to side with Russia against their traditional enemy.

Streltsy infantrymen from Moscow in 1685.

In addition to Russia and Denmark, the most important enemy of the Swedes was represented by the union of Saxony and Poland-Lithuania: the latter countries, were ruled by the same monarch (Augustus II "the Strong"). The Electorate of Saxony was one of the most important and powerful German states from a military point of view; since 1694 it was ruled by Augustus II, a monarch who had great ambitions. In 1697, after the death of the Polish king John III Sobieski (the saviour of Vienna in 1683), Augustus became also king of Poland-Lithuania: as a result, two of the largest states in eastern Europe came under control of a single monarch. At that time Poland-Lithuania was a "Commonwealth" (a sort of confederation) formed by two different states: Poland and Lithuania. Both countries had their own institutions and armies, which were united by the sacred person of the king. Both Poland and Lithuania, however, contained political limitations: the real holders of power in Poland were the great nobles, who were extremely jealous of their autonomy and who always tried to limit the absolute power of the king; Lithuania, for instance, was ravaged during the last years of the 17th century by a cruel civil war fought between two different factions of nobles. One of the two sides was led by the powerful Sapieha family, which controlled some key positions in the Lithuanian Army. In 1698 the Lithuanian civil war temporarily ended thanks to the signing of a new peace treaty; in 1701, however, the

Sapieha family decided to abandon Augustus II and joined Charles XII of Sweden in order to obtain complete control over Lithuania. Augustus hoped to make the Polish-Lithuanian throne hereditary within his family and to use his Saxon military forces to restore order in the Commonwealth (by reducing the power of the local nobles). The outbreak of the war in 1700 prevented him from putting these reforms into practice, something that caused him many troubles during the long conflict. The Polish-Lithuanian Commonwealth provided little in terms of military contribution to Augustus, who had to rely on his loyal Saxons to continue the long and deadly fight against the Swedes. Poland and Lithuania were the battleground over which great parts of the Great Northern War was fought, with the Polish and Lithuanian soldiers playing a limited role.

Finally, the alliance formed against Sweden was completed by two German states: Prussia and Hanover. The Prussians were still a secondary power at the time, but the participation to the Great Northern War transformed their country into a significant regional power. The Duchy of Prussia originated in 1525 from the former State of the Teutonic Order: in that year the knights became Lutheran Protestants and completely secularized their state. Formally, Prussia was a vassal state of Poland. The Duchy was ruled by the Hohenzollern family, whose members already controlled the Margraviate of Brandenburg (a German state centred on Berlin). In 1701 Frederick I Hohenzollern, grandfather of Frederick the Great, elevated Brandenburg-Prussia from Duchy to Kingdom thanks to his alliances with the Holy Roman Empire and Poland. The military reforms that were made during the Great Northern War transformed the Prussian Army into one of the best in Europe, capable to fight in the Baltic area as well as in the Spanish Succession War. At the outbreak of the Great Northern War, Hanover did not exist fully formed: there were, instead, the Duchy of Hanover-Calenberg and the Duchy of Lunenburg-Celle (ruled by two related noble families). In 1705 the two small states were united to form the single Duchy of Hanover, which soon became a significant minor power among the principalities of the Holy Roman Empire. Due to the military support given to the Empire on various occasions, Hanover was transformed into an Electorate in 1708; in 1714 the ruler of Hanover, George Louis, became King of Great Britain after the death of Queen Anne and thus he initiated the personal union between Hanover and Great Britain. Like Prussia, Hanover joined the coalition formed against Sweden with the ambition to conquer the rich Swedish territories that were located in northern Germany.

Reply of the Zaporizhian Cossacks by Ilja Repin. St Petersburg Museum

Sweden had a few allies to rely on during the Great Northern War: the small Duchy of Holstein-Gottorp (located just south of Denmark, formally a vassal state of the Danish kings but effectively a loyal ally of Sweden) and the Ukrainian Cossacks (organized into a sort of "modern" state, known as "Cossack Hetmanate" or "Zaporizhian Host"). At the outbreak of the Great Northern War, the Holstein region of northern Germany was divided in two parts: the southern one was ruled as an independent state by the House of Gottorp, while the northern one was part of Denmark. The dukes of Holstein-Gottorp were, at least formally, "vassals" of the Danish Crown. During the second half of the 17th century, in order to have an ally on Denmark's southern border, the Swedish monarchs created a series of alliances with the rulers of Holstein-Gottorp (using marriages as diplomatic tools). As a result, by 1700 the small German duchy was strongly contested between the two major Scandinavian powers.

In 1649, after bloody and long military campaigns fought against the Poles, the Cossacks of Ukraine finally gained semi-independence and organized themselves into a new state: very soon, however, the Cossack Hetmanate was menaced by the expansionism of Russia. With the ascendancy of Peter the Great, the vast plains of their country became one of Russia's main expansionist targets. As a result of this situation, Ivan Mazepa (the "Hetman" or supreme leader of the Cossacks) decided to side with Sweden in 1708.

Finally, it should be remembered that Sweden was briefly allied with the Ottoman Empire during the years 1710-1714: like the Cossacks, the Ottomans feared Russian expansionism and wanted to defend their Balkan possessions. These comprised three semi-autonomous states, which were under nominal Ottoman control but that effectively acted as independent countries: the Principality of Moldavia, the Principality of Wallachia and the Crimean Khanate. The two Danubian Principalities covered most of modern Romania and were frequently involved into the major wars that were fought in eastern Europe: the great military clashes between the Turks and the Poles, for example, usually took place across their territory.

The Crimean Khanate was the last remnant of the Mongol presence in Russia and Ukraine: after the fall of the Golden Horde during the last decades of the 15th century, Crimea remained in the hands of the Mongols and survived as an independent khanate. In order to resist Polish and Russian expansionism, however, this small tribal state was soon obliged to accept formal Ottoman suzerainty in 1475. The Mongols of Crimea continued to be very active as raiders and slave-traders during the following centuries, obtaining many benefits from Ottoman protection. They were very frequently at war with and against the Cossacks of Ukraine, who controlled a much larger territory; during the Great Northern War, however, the Tatars (Mongols) of Crimea and the Cossacks fought on the same side as they had already done in 1648-1649 against Poland-Lithuania.

By 1720-1721, after having been fighting for two decades against so many enemies, the Swedes became politically and financially exhausted and thus started to conclude separate peace treaties with the various states that made up the enemy coalition; according to these, the whole "Swedish Empire" was divided among the victors. Karelia, Ingria, Estonia and Livonia were given to Russia; the Duchy of Bremen and Verden was occupied by Hanover; the southern part of Western Pomerania was absorbed by Brandenburg-Prussia; the Duchy of Holstein-Gottorp had to cede its northern part to Denmark and to accept the formal suzerainty of the Danish Crown. In addition to Finland (which was abandoned by the Russians who had temporarily occupied it during the conflict), Sweden retained just some little territories in northern Germany (the northern part of Western Pomerania and Wismar).

The Russian Army of Peter the Great, 1696-1725

The Russian military forces in 1696

When Peter the Great became the sole ruler of Russia in 1696, the Tsarist Army functioned as it had for over three hundred years. Compared to western standards it was very old-fashioned and had a completely different organization from the usual one of the European armies of the time. Russia was still a feudal state, with little direct contacts with the rest of the world; commerce was very limited, and the social classes were divided according to a very strict hierarchy. This situation was changed by the revolutionary reforms of Peter, which were all based on the general principle of "looking towards the West". The ambition of the new Tsar was that of transforming all Russian institutions into "westernized" ones, to face the needs of the modern world.

Of all the sectors affected by the reforms of Peter, the military was the one that saw the most dramatic changes. Russia had enormous natural resources and a great number of inhabitants: all this potential, however, had never been fully employed from a military point of view because of technological and logistical difficulties. Before the reforms of the early 18th century, the Russian people was not used to regular military service: for the lowest social classes it was a feudal obligation, while the nobles had little interest in serving as officers in the army or navy. Despite the presence of this widespread mentality, Peter was able to achieve incredible results in an extremely short period of time. After being routed by the Swedes at the Battle of Narva in 1700, by working with incredible determination, the Tsar completely reorganized his military forces: just a few years later, at the Battle of Poltava in 1709, the "new" Russian Army crushed the elite Swedish troops and surprised all the major powers of Europe. The main ambition of Peter was that of conquering a "window to the West" for Russia, an outlet to the Baltic Sea across which his country could gain commerce with the rest of the world. He achieved this by 1721.

Before the ascendancy of Peter the Great, the Russian Army comprised four categories of troops: the "regular" infantry of the Streltsy, some regiments of "foreign" infantry, the heavy cavalry provided by the nobility (pomestnoye voysko) and the irregular light cavalry provided by the Cossacks and allied peoples. The Streltsy were the only component of the Russian Army that showed some elements of regularity and modernity: they had been formed by Tsar Ivan the Terrible around 1550 and were characterized since their origins by the widespread use of firearms (something completely new for the Russian military of the 16th century). With the progression of time, service in the Streltsy units became lifelong and hereditary; as a result, these soldiers soon became a distinct component of Russian society. Different from the previous incarnations of Russian infantrymen, the Streltsy had a proper organization that was based on regiments and were well equipped: in some ways they mirrored the Ottoman Janissaries in their role within society. The various regiments were distinguished according to their provenience: the units from Moscow were known as "Elective Streltsy" while those from other cities were called "Municipal Streltsy". The regiments stationed in the capital were a real elite, being a sort of "Praetorian Guard" that garrisoned the Kremlin fortress and protected the Russian monarchs. They acted also as policemen and firemen for the city and gradually assumed a very important role in politics. Their presence in Moscow meant that they could easily depose a Tsar and elect a new one, thus giving them an enormous importance.

The regiments of Streltsy (*polki*) were divided into "hundreds" (*sotni*); these, in turn, were divided into "tens" (*desyatki*). A distinctive feature of their equipment was the use of poll axes or bardiches; these were used both as weapons and as supports for the muskets when the latter were fired. The Streltsy became a sort of "soldiers-farmers", since the central government often paid them only with the concession of some land. They lived in separate communities, which inhabited specific neighbourhoods or districts; many of them took up secondary sources of income as artisans or merchants in their civil life. Being a privileged social group, the Streltsy were usually against any form of modernization; for this reason, they had a very negative opinion of Peter the Great's program of westernization from the beginning. As a result of the above, and in order to have a new regular infantry that could be free from corruption and privileges, the young Tsar soon initiated a policy that had as main objective the gradual disbandment of the Streltsy. At that time there were 22 regiments of Streltsy infantry, most of which (16) were stationed in Moscow; the remaining six were split between the cities of Novgorod and Pskov (three in each city). To reduce the Streltsy in his capital, Peter initially transferred eight regiments from Moscow to other cities (Belgorod, Sevsk and Kiev); this measure, however, increased the hostility of the Streltsy towards the new regime. In 1698 there was the so-called "Streltsy Revolt", which ended with the total defeat of these elite soldiers: all the regiments from Moscow were disbanded, while those of "Municipal Streltsy" were gradually absorbed into the new "westernized" infantry created by Peter the Great (becoming the backbone of the new units, which were mostly formed by new recruits with no military experience).

Streltsy infantryman from the 1690s.

The "foreign" infantry of the Russian Army was the result of a failed general reform, which had been attempted by the father of Peter the Great (the Tsar Alexis): it was known as "foreign" not because its members came from outside Russia, but because it was organized along contemporary European lines and not as the traditional Streltsy. The original plan of Alexis was very ambitious: he, in fact, had been able to raise a force of 80,000 conscripts with the objective of forming a large body of "modern" infantry. Practical difficulties, political issues and internal oppositions soon led to the failure of his reform: of all the new units that had been planned (63 in total), only two "foreign" infantry regiments were actually formed and thus inherited by Peter the Great. Both were commanded by true foreigners: the "First Moscow" Regiment was under command of Francis Lefort, while the "Boutyrsk" Regiment was at the orders of Patrick Gordon.

Before the military reforms of Peter the Great, the Russian cavalry consisted of noble "heavy" cavalry and Cossack light cavalry; the first was known as *Pomestnoe* and was raised by feudal obligation. The heavy cavalry component was provided by the provincial and urban aristocrats, who were rich enough to have full military equipment and a war horse; the quality of these troops, however, was generally very scarce because the Russian nobles lacked training and modern weapons. For the Narva campaign of 1700 Peter the Great had to rely on the traditional "noble" cavalry, since he had no time to form new "westernized" units as he did for the infantry. The total Russian "traditional" cavalry assembled for the campaign of 1700 comprised 10,000 horsemen. Each noble was generally accompanied by a certain number of armed and mounted retainers, in perfect "feudal" style. The richest aristocrats generally had their places taken by paid replacements coming from their estates. The urban nobles from Moscow were considered to be an elite among the other contingents of aristocrat "heavy" cavalry. Traditionally the Russian noble cavalry was structured on three divisions: one from Moscow, one from Smolensk (assembling the nobles of central Russia) and one from Novgorod (assembling the nobles of northern Russia).

During the Great Northern War, the Russian light cavalry consisted mostly of Cossacks and other "irregular" troops, since Peter the Great paid no great attention to the creation of regular mounted units having light equipment. The immense population of the Russian Empire comprised multiple groups of peoples of different social organizations and living in areas that were quite isolated from one another. These ethnic

Modern artistic representation of a Streltsy regiment on the march.

minorities, which could be quite numerous, and which could still be nomadic, many of which were called "Cossacks" had settled on the frontier areas of the Russian Empire but there also were peoples coming from the Caucasus or from Central Asia with their own peculiar political structures.

Originally the Cossacks were oppressed serfs and outlaws who escaped from the territories under Tsarist control in order to form independent communities on unclaimed lands, which were located in southern Russia and Ukraine. As time progressed, thanks to the great quality of their light cavalry, the Cossacks became a valuable military ally of Russia (especially in the wars against the Crimean Tatars, who were settled in southern Ukraine). At the time of Peter the Great the Cossacks were gradually coming under the political influence of Tsarist Russia, but they still retained a large autonomy. The Cossack communities were structured on regional "Hosts" or "Armies", which were quite independent from the centralized Russian Army. Each Host was stationed in a precise area of the Empire and its military units could be employed away from home only in case of full mobilization.

The Don Host, whose home territory was located between south-eastern Ukraine and the north-western Caucasus, was the most powerful of all. The Bashkir Host was one of the last to adopt some form of proper organization, since its members - the Bashkirs, who were not Cossacks per se - lived on the Russian lands bordering with northern Kazakhstan and followed a lifestyle that had changed very little since the days of Gengis Khan. Wearing chainmail and being armed with composite bows, they impressed the European enemies of Russia much more than the Cossacks. The irregular forces of the Cossacks and of the various nomadic peoples could provide some impressive light cavalry contingents to the Russian military authorities. These units were sometimes criticised by the Russian commanders because they lacked discipline and were equipped with old-fashioned weapons, but in reality, the Cossacks and the other irregulars were the best light cavalry of the world for conducting scouting or skirmishing operations. From an organizational point of view, each Cossack Host fielded a different number of "regiments", which were military units corresponding to administrative subdivisions of the territory. Each Cossack regiment comprised a certain number of "sotnias" ("hundreds") that were in turn divided into "kurins" ("troops") of 25-50 men each. Basically "sotnias" comprised 100 Cossacks, but in many cases, they consisted of up to 200 men.

The "westernization" of the infantry

Even before becoming Tsar, Peter had started to work at the formation of a modern army for his country. In 1682 the young heir to the throne had moved together with his mother to the lodge of Preobrazhenskoe (today part of Moscow), in order to be protected from the political intrigues that took place in the Kremlin. In his new residence the future Tsar gradually formed a small "miniature army", which could help him in the process of learning military art. This small corps was called "Poteshnyi", which literally means "amusement force": in fact, it was created to perform military games and simulations of war. The interesting thing, however, was

The Russian Army of 1696 - 1796

(Top Left) Grenadier officer of the Guard infantry from the reign of Peter the Great. The headgear, made of black leather, was used only by the grenadiers of the Imperial Guard's infantry.

(Top Right) Musketeer officer of the Guard infantry from the reign of Peter the Great. The golden lace and the decorative embroidering on the buttonholes were peculiar of the Imperial Guard's infantry.

(Bottom Left) Musketeer NCO of the line infantry from the reign of Peter the Great. The standard uniform shown here was very simple, being dark green with red facings.

(Bottom Right) Trooper of the dragoons from the reign of Peter the Great. Until the end of the Great Northern War, some dragoon regiments were dressed in white and not dark green.

that this miniature army had all the main features of a modern European army (firearms, training, discipline, organization, equipment, tactics and uniforms). The original members of this small army were children, servants and retainers who were all linked to the small court of the young Peter. Initially the "Poteshnyi" consisted of just one company with 100 "bombardiers"; the use of the latter term derived from the fact that they had two artillery pieces at their disposal. By 1685 there were 300 bombardiers at Preobrazhenskoe; later, when their number was increased to 600, a second company was formed and garrisoned in the nearby village of Semyonovskoe. With the progression of time, the quality of the "Poteshnyi" increased a lot due to the employment of foreign officers as military advisers: one of these, the already mentioned Patrick Gordon, became the commander of Peter's miniature army.

On 25 April 1695, shortly before becoming absolute ruler of Russia, the future Tsar decided that the time had come to transform his personal army into proper military units: after a significant enlargement that was made possible by the arrival of new recruits, the original two companies became the "Preobrazhenskoe" Regiment and the "Semyonovskoe" Regiment (respectively the 1st and 2nd regiment of the new Russian Imperial Guard). These units soon became the core of Peter's new "westernized" infantry. Originally each of the two regiments had 12 companies of 100 men; four companies were assembled together to form a battalion and thus each regiment had three battalions. The "Preobrazhenskoe" Regiment also had an additional "Bombardier Company", equipped with six mortars and four field guns.

Grenadier private (left) and NCO (right) of the "Preobrazhenskoe" Regiment, wearing the uniform that was used during 1742-1762. The grenadiers of the Imperial Guard's foot regiments had a peculiar headgear decorated with many coloured feathers; note the golden piping on the collar and cuffs of the NCO.

In 1700 the "Preobrazhenskoe" Regiment was increased to four battalions; in 1704 a "Grenadier Company" was added to both units. Initially most of the two Guard regiments' officers were foreigners, who had been former military advisors of the "Poteshnyi"; their members, instead, were mostly young nobles who received their military instruction in these corps before becoming officers. In 1698 both units played a key role in the suppression of the "Streltsy Revolt", thus acting as the real "guardians" of Peter the Great and of his reforms.

In November 1699 a proclamation was published in all Russia, calling for volunteers to form a new national army. This would have comprised infantry regiments organized according to the new model which was already practiced in the two units of the Imperial Guard. All the peasants enlisted in the new army would have been freed from their condition of serfs; for the latter reason the proclamation proved to be very alluring for thousands of volunteers, but this was not enough to form a new army. As a result, Peter the Great ordered

Musketeer NCO of the "Preobrazhenskoe" Regiment (left), private of the "Semyonovskoe" Regiment (centre) and private of the "Izmailovsky" Regiment (right). They are all wearing the uniform that was used during 1742-1762.

the conscription of serfs in all the territories of Russia: each parish of the Orthodox Church would have to provide 25 recruits, while each secular noble owning from 30 to 50 farms would have provided one recruit for each farm owned. As a result of these measures, an enormous mass of potential soldiers arrived during the early months of 1700 at Peter's main military base of Preobrazhenskoe. A total of 32,000 recruits were assigned to the infantry and were organized into 27 regiments; these were in turn assembled into three large divisions with nine regiments each.

After a few months of partial training, these largely unexperienced regiments had to face the Swedish veterans at the Battle of Narva: the result was a real disaster, but the process initiated by Peter the Great was the correct one. After Narva, the new Russian Army had several years to organize itself in a proper way and to acquire more battlefield experience; training and discipline were improved, while the military operations conducted on secondary fronts increased the morale of the recruits. From 1704 to 1706 the Russian Army lent one of its divisions to Augustus II of Saxony to fight against Charles XII in Poland. In this case the operations against the Swedes ended as a complete disaster for the Russians, but while this happened on the main front the Tsar was able to forge a new and formidable military machine. Between 1701 and 1708 the Russian infantry saw a very rapid expansion: the original 27 regiments were increased to 56, plus 5 regiments formed exclusively with grenadier companies.

Grenadiers emerged as a new troop type of the European infantry during the second half of the 17th century, when the various armies started to employ hand-grenades as a new weapon. The latter could be thrown by infantrymen and were quite simple to produce; they, in addition, could be of great use during siege operations as well as be employed during pitched battles to destroy enemy field fortifications. In order to use the new weapon in an effective way, the various infantry units of the European armies started to select the tallest and strongest men among their members; these were re-trained as grenadiers and learned how to use hand-grenades on the battlefield. The French Army was the first to create some independent sub-units of grenadiers inside its infantry regiments, since in 1671 a company of grenadiers was included in each infantry battalion. During the following decades grenadiers soon became the elite of the French foot troops, thanks to their superior training and discipline; as time progressed, the French innovations were adopted also by the other European armies and thus grenadiers could be found practically everywhere in the continent. Many monarchs later transformed their units of grenadiers into elite corps having "guard" status and thus this new category of "heavy infantry" became increasingly popular.

The new infantry regiments of Peter the Great were organized quite similarly to the "foreign" units of his father Alexis (the "First Moscow" Regiment and the "Boutyrsk" Regiment). The latter had 1,200 men assembled into eight companies of 150 men each; the traditional Streltsy infantry, instead, had been organized into regiments of 2,000 soldiers each. The new regiments formed in 1699-1700 had two battalions with five companies each; a single company had 100 men. Only four of the original 27 regiments had a higher establishment with three battalions instead of two. A battery of two 3-pdr guns was attached to each regiment. In 1704 the five companies of each battalion were organized as one company of grenadiers and four of musketeers; in 1708 the grenadier companies of each infantry unit (except for those of two regiments) were detached to form the five independent grenadier regiments. During that same year all the infantry regiments started to be known by the name of their home provinces or towns and not by the name of their commanding colonels. In 1716 there was the last significant organizational change: the "Preobrazhenskoe" Regiment of the Imperial Guard was reduced to three battalions, while the number of line regiments having three battalions each instead of two was reduced to one.

From 1712 the Russian infantry started to include some new garrison regiments, which were specifically formed to be stationed in the newly-conquered territories of the Baltic. Peter the Great, in fact, did not want to use his line units for performing passive garrison duties. These new regiments were also used in Russia, to act as "police forces" against internal uprisings (especially revolts of the Cossacks). In total, 39 of such units were formed; in addition to the infantry corps, there were also two regiments and one squadron of cavalry "garrison dragoons". By 1716 the garrison infantry had been expanded with the formation of another ten regiments and one independent battalion. The garrison cavalry was increased, being now composed by four regiments and one independent squadron of dragoons. The principal duties of the garrison troops combined the roles of police and border guards; they, however, also assisted in collecting taxes and in the recruitment of new soldiers as well as in the rounding up of deserters. The garrison soldiers were paid by raising revenue for their upkeep from within their military district. They were tasked with keeping an eye on the Cossack communities as well as with preventing the outbreak of peasant revolts. For garrisoning that portion of Ukraine that came under Russian control after the Battle of Poltava, Peter the Great ordered the creation of a separate militia: on 2 February 1713 this "Ukrainian Land Militia" was organized and gradually came to comprise six infantry regiments, each having ten companies. All the members of these units were free yeomen and non-Cossacks.

Uniforms of the Infantry

According to Knötel the uniform was a long western style coat, a long waist coat, knee breeches, stockings and shoes. The cap had flaps to cover the ears in cold weather. The uniform colors were left up to the colonel.

Regiment	Coat	Lining	Breeches/Waistcoat	Grenadiers
Preobrazhenskoe	Dark Green	Dark Red	Dark Green	Black leather cap
Semenov	Light Blue	Dark Red	Dark Green	Black leather cap

After 1720 the caps were replaced by hats. The Line infantry adopted dark green coats with collar, cuffs breeches and waistcoat in red, with white stockings. The guard regiments wore dark green coats, waistcoats and breeches. The cuffs, lining and lace were red. The Preobrazhenskoe had red collars and the Semenov had light blue.

The Reform of the Cavalry

After his noble cavalry abandoned the field without fighting at Narva, Peter the Great understood that he had to intervene on the organization of the mounted troops as he had already done for the infantry. Something had already been attempted before the Battle of Narva: after the recruits of the new army were assembled at Preobrazhenskoye, Peter the Great had ordered the formation of two dragoon regiments that were both put under command of two foreign officers. The first units of dragoons appeared in the European armies during the last phase of the Thirty Years' War, the bloody conflict that ravaged most of Germany during

Trooper of the "Cavalier-Guards", wearing the first uniform of his corps that was issued in 1723. Note the red richly-embroidered "soubreveste" that was worn over the coat, which was typical of mounted bodyguards during the 18th century.

the years 1618-1648. The basic idea behind the formation of the first dragoon corps was that of having some soldiers who could move on horses but fight on foot. The armies of the time, in fact, increasingly needed highly mobile troops that could travel long distances in a short time but that could also fight as standard infantry when needed. As a result, the first companies of dragoons were organized to face these specific tactical needs: they consisted of ordinary infantrymen who knew how to ride a horse and who could perform as a sort of "mounted infantry". The same term "dragoons" derived from the multi-tasking nature of these new soldiers: like the mythical beasts giving them their name, capable of living on earth as well as on water, the dragoons could be employed as infantrymen but also as cavalrymen.

Dragoons were widely used in the Polish-Lithuanian armies in the middle of the 17th century and were increasingly organized by western armies in the late 17th century. Initially these new corps had much more in common with the infantry than with the cavalry: they did not wear boots like the ordinary mounted troops, they were organized into companies and not into squadrons, their musicians were drummers and not trumpeters, their main weapon was an infantry musket and not a cavalry sword. With the progression of time, however, the dragoons partly changed their tactical nature since they started to be employed as mounted infantrymen less frequently. On most occasions they were asked to act as proper cavalry, being tasked with conducting frontal charges and other tactical functions that were typical of the mounted "shock" troops. The dragoons gradually became a sort of "medium cavalry": as a result, they could attack the enemy with a frontal charge but could also conduct skirmishing operations in open order.

The first two "westernized" units of the Russian cavalry did not perform well during the 1700 campaign, but they showed good capabilities in scouting and foraging. As a result, in 1701, a total of 12 new dragoon regiments were added to the two original ones. Another six regiments were formed during the following years: three during 1702-1703 and another three in 1705. The expansion continued in a very speedy way: by 1709, in fact, the Russian Army comprised 37 cavalry regiments (34 of dragoons and 3 of horse grenadiers). The original two regiments had ten companies of 100 men each; two companies were assembled to form a squadron of 200 soldiers and thus each regiment had five squadrons. In 1704 all the existing dragoon regiments were reorganized on 12 companies each, which were divided into four squadrons of three companies.

In 1705 a company of horse grenadiers was added to each dragoon regiment, which was formed by assembling together the best veterans of each unit. In 1708 all the horse grenadier companies of the army were detached from their parent units and assembled together in order to form three new regiments of elite horse grenadiers. In 1710 the internal organization of all cavalry regiments was again reverted to 10 companies. Until 1719, Peter the Great had no cavalry units inside his elite Imperial Guard. Starting in 1704, however, the two leading commanders of the Russian Army started to be protected by chosen cavalry units that acted as their mounted bodyguards: these were the "Life Squadron" of Prince Menshikov and the "General's Dragoon Company" of Count Sherematiev. These two corps were proper line cavalry ones and not dragoon units;

Trooper of the dragoons from the reign of Peter the Great. He is wearing the winter cap with ear flaps that was much more popular than the black tricorn during cold months.

they were almost entirely composed by young officers, who wanted to earn some combat experience and to have an opportunity to show their personal valour. In 1706 also the governor of the newly founded city of Saint Petersburg - which was chosen by the Tsar as the new capital of Russia - was given a dragoon company, which performed police duties in the new urban centre. In 1719 the Tsar ordered the amalgamation of these three independent squadron-sized units, in order to form a "Life Guard" Cavalry Regiment. This was to be part of the Imperial Guard and soon became a "training unit" for young officers, who were sent to command dragoon regiments after serving in its ranks. Already in 1721, however, the "Life Guard" Cavalry Regiment was disbanded and its members were used to form a new dragoon regiment.

When a large uprising - the "Bulavin Rebellion" - broke out among the Don Cossacks in 1707, Peter the Great decided that it was necessary to form a regular light cavalry corps since the Cossacks had proved to be too much unreliable; this was organized using the Hungarian hussars of the Austrian Army as the model. The latter became famous during the early years of the 18th century for their excellent combat performances in the War of the Spanish Succession. Since the 1550's, the light horsemen from Hungary known as "hussars" gradually started to introduce a new form of mobile warfare. The etymology of the word "hussar" is not very clear and during past years several theories have been elaborated in order to explain how this term came to indicate the light cavalrymen of Hungary. Most of the etymologists and historians, however, agree on the fact that the word could come from the Hungarian "huszár"; the latter term was a modified version of the medieval Serbian "husar", a word that was used to indicate the "mounted brigands" who harassed the peasant communities living in the countryside of the Balkan nations.

In 1526 the expanding Ottoman Empire of the Turks defeated and invaded the large Kingdom of Hungary, which had been one of the leading political and military powers of Eastern Europe during the Middle Ages. The Ottomans occupied most of the Hungarian lands, but not the region of Transylvania that retained a certain degree of autonomy. During the second half of the XVI century the territory of Hungary became the main battleground for the bloody wars that took place between the Habsburg Empire and the Ottoman Empire; these conflicts, which continued for most of the following century, were mostly fought for possession of Hungary since the Habsburgs were strongly determined to cancel the Turkish presence in the northern Balkans (which represented a serious threat to the political stability of their Austrian homeland). Initially the Ottomans obtained a series of victories during these wars, but with the progression of time the Habsburgs gained the upper hand. By the end of the XVII century parts of Transylvania had been annexed to the Austrian Empire together with some other Hungarian territories; in addition, the Habsburgs had started to exert their political control also over Croatia (the latter had been a vassal state of

Bombardier of the artillery from the reign of Peter the Great. The headgear, made of black leather, was used only by the bombardiers since the other artillerymen had a standard black tricorn.

A 19th century artistic representation of Tsar Peter the Great

Hungary for most of the Middle Ages).

During the XVII century the Balkans were always at war, since both the Habsburgs and the Turks employed bands of irregulars to conduct raids across their respective borders also when there was no "official conflict" going on. These irregulars, perceived as simple "brigands" by the local communities, acted in a very autonomous way and had no military discipline to speak of. They pillaged the frontier territories of their enemies and killed civilians with no mercy, earning a living as real "land pirates".

These early hussars were not paid for their "services" but were of great use for the Habsburgs and for the Ottomans, who could maintain a "state of war" on the Balkan frontier without deploying their regular troops in that theatre of operations (something that had significant economic costs). The harsh nature of the local terrain and the tactical duties that they had to perform made the hussars a very peculiar category of mounted troops: in order to move very rapidly on the hills and in the woods of the Balkans to conduct their "guerrilla operations", in fact, they had to be mounted on agile but sturdy horses and had to carry a light equipment consisting of offensive weapons only. With the progression of time, the Habsburgs tried to partly "regularize" their bands of hussars recruited from Hungary and Croatia; they, in fact, understood that these mounted skirmishers could be of great use also in other theatres of operations located outside the Balkans.

In the early decades of the XVII century the hussars started to add light firearms to their equipment and a good number of them – mostly coming from Croatia – were employed in Central Europe by their Habsburg masters during the Thirty Years' War. Both the Austrians and their opponents were greatly impressed by the combat capabilities of the hussars, who were able to conduct reconnaissance missions in a very effective way as well as to harass enemy columns by using "hit-and-run" tactics. France, one of Austria's main enemies during the Thirty Years' War, was one of the first European nations to recruit some contingents of Hungarian and Croatian mercenaries for service inside her military forces.

By the beginning of the 18th century the Austrian Army comprised several regular regiments of hussar light cavalry, which performed with distinction during the War of the Spanish Succession. It was these Hungarian units that Peter the Great choose as a model for the regular light cavalry that he tried to form. The latter consisted of a single squadron, numbering 300 men in total; these were recruited from the Christian inhabitants of several Balkan countries (Hungary, Serbia, Moldavia and Wallachia). The unit was commanded by a Wallachian nobleman and was stationed on the Russian border with the Ottoman Empire, in order to act as a sort of "special" garrison unit. Shortly before launching a military campaign against the Ottomans in 1711, the Tsar increased the Russian regular light cavalry to six full regiments of hussars; each of these was to have four squadrons with 200 men, thus deploying a total of 800 horsemen. During the 1711 campaign, however, the new light regiments gave a quite negative account of themselves (especially in terms of discipline); as a result, when the short war with the Ottomans ended, they were all disbanded except for two regiments that were retained in service until 1721. The first experiment aimed at creating a regular light cavalry inside the Russian Army had failed, mostly because of the presence and availability of large numbers of Cossack contingents; the long history of the Russian hussars, however, had just began.

Uniforms of the Cavalry

In 1700, the dragoon uniforms were left up to the colonels of the regiments. After 1720, regiments adopted blue coats with white linings and lace. They also had leather waistcoat and breeches.

Artillery and naval infantry

In the late 17th century, most of the European states were still in the process of organizing their own artillery units in a proper way. Several armies, including the Russian one, did not contain any permanent company/battery of artillery: temporary artillery trains were organized only when needed by assembling together all the available field pieces and were usually disbanded at the end of each campaign. The few professional artillerymen available in Russia at the beginning of Peter's reign were scattered across the country and were mostly tasked with manning the guns of the various garrisons. In time of war, they were required to fire their guns but were not equipped to defend themselves from enemy attacks; as a result, while on the battlefield, they had to be "escorted" by some infantrymen. In the field, the artillerymen were supplemented with the needed number of civilian matrosses and pioneers, the latter being semi-skilled civilian labourers who were contracted only for the duration of a campaign. The conductors of the carts that were used to move the artillery pieces were all civilians.

Before the defeat of Narva, the Russian Army did not have a proper artillery corps but just an artillery train that comprised several pieces produced in the Kremlin fortress under the technical supervision of foreign experts. Similarly to what happened in other European armies, however, all line infantry units had a regimental artillery section consisting of two guns and the two infantry regiments of the Imperial Guard had their own artillery pieces (six mortars and four field guns for the "Preobrazhensky" Regiment and six field guns for the "Semyonovsky" Regiment). An elite "Company of Bombardiers" was attached to the "Preobrazhensky" Regiment. In 1701 all the Russian field guns were grouped into batteries, which were distinguished according to their tactical employment (field artillery, fortress artillery or siege artillery). In that same year an independent "Regiment of Artillery" was created, which was structured as follows: one company of bombardiers, six companies of cannoniers, one company of miners, a detachment of engineers, a detachment of pontonniers/pioneers and a detachment of petardiers. Bombardiers served howitzers and mortars, while the cannoniers served field guns. The bombardiers were also equipped with hand mortars rested on special halberds that could fire powerful grenades. The new composite "artillery" unit of the Russian Army soon proved to be of excellent quality, due to the fact that it underwent some intensive training that was conducted under the supervision of foreign officers. Despite the creation of the "Artillery Regiment", the old system of regimental artillery continued to exist. It is important to remember that the artillery reform of Peter the Great was made possible thanks to the fundamental role played by a Scottish artillery specialist, James William Bruce, who served the ambitious Tsar with competence and loyalty.

The Great Northern War marked the birth also of another "specialist" unit of the Russian Army: the naval infantry. Until the ascendancy of Peter the Great, Russia had no proper military fleet to speak of; as a result, there were no units of naval infantry. During the first years of the conflict, the Tsar assigned three line infantry regiments to the fleet: these were used on several occasions for amphibious operations and soon showed all their valour and utility in battle. Bearing in mind these good results, in 1705 Peter the Great ordered the creation of an autonomous "Regiment of Naval Infantry", which should have been assigned to the Russian Navy. The new unit was created with the best soldiers of the Russian line infantry and its officers were taken from the experienced NCOs of the Imperial Guard infantry regiments. The naval infantry performed extremely well during the rest of the Great Northern War and thus became very soon an elite unit of the

Russian military.

Uniforms of the Artillery

The artillery uniforms had red coats, waistcoats and breeches. The cuffs and linings were cornflower blue. The gunners wore a leather cap similar to the grenadiers.

The Russian Army of Empress Anna, 1730-1740

The Imperial Guard

Until 1730 the infantry of the Russian Imperial Guard comprised two corps: the "Preobrazhensky" Regiment and the "Semyonovsky" Regiment, no doubt the best infantry units of the Russian Army due to their excellent discipline and firm loyalty towards the Tsar. Both regiments earned a solid military reputation in a few years. After Peter the Great's death in 1725 they spent most of their time in the Russian capital of Saint Petersburg where they acted as elite garrison troops, while their officers played a prominent role in some court intrigues. The officers of the Imperial Guard's infantry regiments came from the most important aristocratic families of Russia, but also the NCOs and privates of the two units were mostly noblemen (coming from families of the lesser nobility). Until 1727 the Russian Imperial Guard was commanded by Prince Menshikov, Peter the Great's favourite military commander; in that year, however, Menshikov was removed by the new Tsar Peter II since the latter feared that he could organize a military coup to increase his personal power.

The Imperial Guard consisted of men who influenced the political life of Russia and thus always had its interests well represented in the court. The removal of Menshikov was perceived as an offence by most of the guardsmen and thus – to avoid problems – Peter II temporarily moved his capital from Saint Petersburg to Moscow. The new Tsar soon proved to be a weak monarch and was not able to establish a positive relationship with his military forces; as a result, following a period of wrangling within the Russian court, he was replaced with Peter the Great's niece Anna. Anna ruled Russia for ten years, but initially had significant limitations to her personal power. The major nobles of the country, in fact, wanted to control her political decisions in order to restore the privileges that they had partly lost under Peter the Great. Anna, however, demonstrated to be very intelligent and won the loyalty of the Imperial Guard. With the decisive support of the "Preobrazhensky" Regiment she mounted a military coup against the aristocrats who wanted to control her actions and restored the imperial powers introduced by Peter the Great.

In 1730, to further safeguard her position inside the Russian court, Anna decided to raise a third foot regiment inside the Imperial Guard. She did so by assembling the best elements of the "Ukrainian Land Militia", which had been created in 1713 by Peter the Great. Since the new corps was mustered for the first time in the city of Izmailovo, it received the official denomination of "Izmailovsky" Regiment. The Izmailovsky, like the two existing foot regiments of the Russian Imperial Guard, consisted of three battalions with three companies of musketeers and one company of grenadiers each. Empress Anna wanted to have a very reliable and loyal Imperial Guard; as a result, she decided to choose the officers for the new Izmailovsky Regiment mostly from German mercenary officers. As we have already seen, the Russian Army had hired significant numbers of foreign "military experts" since the last decades of the 17th century; these professional officers, in fact, had solid competences and were not involved into the political intrigues of the Russian court.

Official portrait of Empress Anna of Russia (who ruled 1730-1740)

During Anna's reign dozens of German officers entered the Russian Army, thus initiating a real process of "Germanification" of the army. The German officers carried on the "westernization" and modernization of the Russian Army that had been initiated by Peter the Great, by introducing effective training and discipline in the ranks of the Russian military forces. Pay and conditions of service were improved, in order to attract volunteers who could be interested in becoming professional soldiers. At the same time, the nobility was partly freed from the strict military obligations that had been introduced by Peter the Great. The process of "Germanification" of the Russian Army continued until the ascendancy of Catherine the Great in 1762, becoming particularly strong after the Prussian Army came to dominate the European battlefields from 1740. For the peasant recruits provided to the army, however, service was a "life" sentence. Those that survived to old age might become a pensioner but never retired.

During the years 1721-1723 the Russian Imperial Guard still did not comprise any cavalry unit; however, this could not last for long since the Tsars needed a corps that could act as their mounted bodyguard. During the Great Northern War Peter the Great, following the example of his Swedish rival Charles XII, raised a squadron of 300 "drabants" or "mounted bodyguards" inside his elite Preobrazhensky Regiment. This new corps followed the Emperor during all his voyages and performed ceremonial duties during formal occasions. By the end of the Great Northern War, however, the squadron had been disbanded for economic reasons. In November 1723, in preparation for the coronation of his wife that was going to take place in Moscow, Peter the Great decided to raise a new company of "drabants" that would have received the official designation of "Cavalier-Guards". The latter was formed by assembling supernumerary senior officers coming from all the units of the Russian Army; it consisted of just 60 horsemen wearing magnificent uniforms, who escorted the ceremonial procession of the imperial family during the coronation of Peter's wife. In May 1724, however, the "Cavalier-Guards" were disbanded since they had been raised as a temporary corps tasked with performing on just one special occasion. In 1725, due to the need for a mounted corps inside the Imperial Guard, the company was re-formed. This time it was re-raised on a permanent basis, but in 1731 it was disbanded by Empress Anna because of its expense to maintain.

The infantry

During the period 1725-1762 the Russian line infantry was progressively expanded with the formation of new units, to the point that by the time of Catherine the Great's ascension to the throne it comprised a total of 46 regiments. Initially each of the latter mustered two battalions and a single battalion comprised four companies of musketeers. An artillery section, equipped with two 3-pdr guns, was attached to each line infantry unit. The number of guns assigned to each regiment had been increased to four by 1730. In 1731 the five independent grenadier regiments that had been created by Peter the Great were disbanded; the best elements of each line infantry unit, however, were assembled together in order to form one new grenadier company in each line infantry battalion. The grenadier companies were larger than the musketeer ones, since they had 200 men each.

During the period 1725-1762 also the "garrison infantry" of the Russian Army was significantly enlarged. By the time of Catherine the Great's ascension to the throne it consisted of 47 regiments and 4 battalions, which were assembled into two separate organizations: the "Ostsee Garrison Infantry" and the "Inner Garrison Infantry". The first consisted of those regiments and battalions that were stationed in the area of the Baltic, whose main function was to counter foreign invasions of the Russian territory by defending the most important fortresses; the second consisted of those regiments and battalions that were stationed into the interior areas of Russia, whose function was to counter internal rebellions by patrolling the major urban centres as well as the countryside. The "Ostsee Garrison Infantry" mustered 20 regiments numbered from 1 to 20 plus a single independent battalion; the "Inner Garrison Infantry" mustered 27 regiments numbered from 21 to 47 plus three independent battalions (one of these battalions had a special status, since it acted

(Left) Musketeer of the line infantry, wearing the uniform used during 1756-1762. The general appearance of the Russian line infantrymen had not changed a lot since the days of Peter the Great: black tricorn, dark green coat with red facings, red waistcoat and breeches, white gaiters (black during winter).

(Right) Grenadier officer of the line infantry, wearing the uniform used during 1756-1762. Officers were easy to recognize on the battlefield thanks to some peculiar elements of their dress, like the golden waist-sash and the "gorget" (metal plate) worn under the neck.

(Left) Grenadier of the line infantry, wearing the uniform used during 1756-1762. The "mitre" cap, having brass frontal plate, differentiated grenadiers from musketeers. The grenadier regiments and the grenadier companies of the musketeer regiments wore the same uniform.

(Right) NCO (left) and private (right) of the artillery sections attached to the line infantry regiments, wearing the uniform used during 1756-1762. As clear from this picture, the members of the artillery sections were dressed quite similarly to musketeers.

Grenadiers of the line infantry from the reign of Empress Anna. The uniform had changed very little since the days of Peter the Great, except for the practice of buttoning up the skirts of the coat.

as the municipal guard of Moscow). The internal structure of the garrison infantry regiments was very similar to that of the line infantry ones; it should be noted, however, that during 1731-1741 the garrison infantry regiments did not have grenadier companies. The senior staff of a garrison regiment mustered one colonel, one lieutenant-colonel and one first-major; the junior staff had one quartermaster, one clerk, one supply officer, one surgeon, two provosts, two blacksmiths, two workers and seven oboists. Each of the two battalions that made up a regiment had four musketeer companies and from 1741 contained one grenadier company. A garrison musketeer company comprised the following elements: one captain, one lieutenant, one ensign, one sergeant, one armourer, one standard-bearer, one clerk, one barber, four corporals, two drummers and 120 privates. A garrison grenadier company comprised the following elements: one captain, one lieutenant, one sub-lieutenant, one sergeant, one armourer, one clerk, one barber, four corporals, two drummers and 12 privates. Only one of the garrison regiments - the "Yakutskiy" - had a non-standard internal establishment with three battalions instead of two and with an attached company of horse grenadiers. The senior staff of an independent garrison battalion mustered just one lieutenant-colonel; the junior staff had one clerk, one surgeon, one provost and one worker. Each independent garrison battalion had just four companies of musketeers, with the composition as follows: one captain, one lieutenant, one ensign, one sergeant, one armourer, one standard-bearer, four corporals, two drummers, one clerk, one barber, 16 grenadiers and 120 musketeers. The single independent battalion of the "Ostsee Garrison Infantry" was the only one to have a slightly different internal structure; it performed the specific task of defending the crucial Ladoga Canal that connected the Neva River and the Svir River not far from Saint Petersburg.

The "Ukrainian Land Militia" created by Peter the Great continued to exist after his death and was expanded to muster a total of 20 infantry regiments. It initially comprised large numbers of minor noblemen and former Streltsy who were not absorbed into the new military system established during the Great Northern War but who were still useful because of their combat skills. These individuals were settled as "military colonists" in a series of garrisons that were placed on the frontier line that divided Russia from Ukraine; this long border extended itself from the Dniepr River to the Seversky Donets River, being constantly exposed to the attacks of the Ukrainian Cossacks as well as of the Crimean Tatars. The members of the Ukrainian Land Militia were all "crown peasants", i.e. free individuals who had more personal rights than the serfs who made up most of the regular army's lower ranks. Their regiments consisted of ten musketeer companies each but were largely administrative units since the various companies were scattered throughout Ukraine in defence of many border locations.

Each infantry company comprised 16 grenadiers and could have a small artillery detachment equipped with just one or two guns. Following the example of the Ukrainian Land Militia, in 1736 the Russians created a similar corps also on the Trans-Kama border that divided their territories from the lands of the warlike Bashkirs and Kalmyks. The Trans-Kama border extended itself between the Samara River and the Kama River; it was characterized by an extremely hostile natural environment and thus was not easy to defend.

Dragoon wearing the uniform used during 1756-1762. During Peter the Great's reign the Russian dragoons had been dressed in dark green, but the latter colour was later changed to dark blue.

Dragoon standard-bearer (left) and trooper (right) from the late reign of Peter the Great. Under the latter, some dragoon regiments of the Russian Army were not uniformed in green but in blue.

The "Trans-Kama Land Militia" consisted of one infantry regiment with eight companies and three dragoon regiments with ten companies each; the predominance of cavalry was due to the fact that both the Bashkirs and the Kalmyks fought as mobile light horsemen. Each infantry company included 16 infantry grenadiers, while each dragoon company included 10 horse grenadiers.

The New Heavy Cavalry and the Dragoons

In 1725 the cavalry of the Russian Army, except for that of the Imperial Guard, comprised only regiments of dragoons and regiments of horse grenadiers; no heavy cavalry units of cuirassiers existed, differentiating the Russian mounted troops from those of the contemporary West European armies. "Cuirassiers" per se first appeared in the European armies during the second half of the 16th century, being created to replace the former fully armoured heavy cavalry of the men-at-arms (whose tactics and military traditions went back to the Middle Ages). The introduction of new and smaller firearms that could be employed also on horseback, in fact, gradually led to the replacement of the heavy lance with pistols and swords as the main cavalry weapon. The new European heavy cavalrymen who dominated the battlefields of the Thirty Years' War (1618-1648) were mostly cuirassiers, non-aristocratic mounted fighters who were armed with pistols (in addition to their sword) and who no longer used armour on their limbs. These horsemen soon became known as "cuirassiers", since they wore armour that was reduced only to the cuirass (originally consisting of both breastplate and backplate). By 1660 most of the European armies had modified the panoply of their heavy cavalry contingents: helmets – which had been quite popular until that moment – were gradually phased out together with the backplate of the cuirass. In addition, the pistols lost most of their importance and thus most of the cuirassiers started to be equipped only with a massive sword having straight blade.

Trooper of the "Cavalier-Guards" from the late reign of Peter the Great. The uniform is very similar to that of the contemporary French Royal Musketeers.

The combat experiences of the first half of the 18th century showed to some military commanders that the cuirasses of the heavy cavalry had lost most of their previous protective function, since the new flintlock muskets of the infantry could easily pierce any kind of cuirass from a certain distance. As a result of the above some armies, like the French, transformed their cuirassiers into line cavalry by abolishing the use of breastplates. There were, however, several significant exceptions to this rule: Frederick the Great of Prussia, for example, never deprived his heavy cavalry of cuirasses since he thought that the latter could be of great use during close combat cavalry battles.

During his reign, Peter the Great refused to raise any heavy cavalry regiment of cuirassiers inside the Russian Army since he believed that the dragoon units were the only cavalry corps capable of operating in an effective way on the peculiar territory of eastern Europe. Being mounted infantrymen moving on agile horses, the dragoons were ideal for conducting a variety of different missions: they could perform reconnaissance duties on every kind of terrain and could dismount to support the infantry; if needed, however, they could also charge in close formation like the heavy cavalrymen of other armies. Peter the Great's tactical views regarding heavy cavalry were also determined by some practical factors: in Russia, in fact, only the nobility had the massive horses capable of bearing cuirassiers wearing heavy personal equipment.

Following the Tsar's death and the beginning of the "Germanification" of the Russian Army, Empress Anna started to plan the creation of some heavy cavalry units inside her military forces. As we have already seen, she called many professional German officers to serve in the Russian Army; the most important of these was Baron Burchard Christoph Munnich, who became the senior commander of the Russian military forces in 1732. Munnich gradually re-modelled the Russian Army along contemporary Prussian lines and thus intervened on the composition of the mounted forces. He planned to raise ten regiments of cuirassiers mounted on massive horses of the Holstein breed imported from Germany, which would have acted as the new "shock troops" of the Russian cavalry.

In 1731 the first regiment of cuirassiers was formed by converting one of the existing dragoon units; the new corps became known as "Munnich's Cuirassiers" and acted as a model for all the new heavy cavalry corps that were formed after it. The unit was stationed in Saint Petersburg and consisted of five squadrons with two companies each. Another two regiments of cuirassiers were soon raised after the first, always by converting existing units of dragoons. The three heavy cavalry regiments included several German officers in their commanding staffs but experienced a series of practical problems after their creation; first of all, for example, they suffered from a chronic shortage of suitable mounts and their members had to be completely re-trained. The costs for maintaining in service a cuirassier regiment were exorbitant for the Russian military standards of the time, but Empress Anna wanted to have some reliable mounted units to count on in case the infantry regiments of the Imperial Guard turned against her. For this reason, she spent large sums of money to equip her cuirassiers and conceded several special privileges to them: the new heavy cavalrymen were paid more than any other soldier of the Russian line troops, were always stationed in or around Saint Petersburg and could not be punished with beatings. In 1740 a fourth regiment of cuirassiers was formed by converting a unit of dragoons.

The horse grenadier regiments existing during Peter the Great's reign were all disbanded in 1726, in order to add one company of horse grenadiers to each of the existing dragoon regiments. The horse grenadiers were the elite "shock force" of each dragoon unit, since they were to operate as heavy cavalry during frontal charges or as dismounted grenadiers to form storming parties. As anticipated above, the mainstay of the Russian cavalry during the first half of the 18th century was represented by the dragoon regiments. The latter, being mounted on smaller horses than those employed by the dragoon corps of other European armies, were extremely flexible from a tactical point of view but were not capable of contrasting the heavy cavalry equipped with cuirasses. With the progression of time, it became clear that the original "mounted infantry" character that the Russian dragoons had always retained was no longer of any use on the European battlefields, while it could still be effective during the campaigns conducted by the Russians in Asia. For this reason, as we have already seen, 12 of the 30 dragoon regiments existing in 1725 were progressively transformed into heavy cavalry units of cuirassiers or horse grenadiers.

The Light Cavalry

During the first four decades of the 18th century heavy cavalry was the most important component of the European mounted troops, since it made up the bulk of the cavalry forces mobilized by the various nations and also because it had acquired a certain tactical supremacy on the battlefields of the continent. Highly trained and well-disciplined, it consisted of horsemen armed with long swords having straight blade and mounted on massive horses; these were able to charge and manoeuvre in perfect order by maintaining "knee-to-knee" close formations. This kind of cavalry was mostly employed to conduct frontal charges and to cover the retreat of the line infantry if they were routed by the enemy. Around the time of the Thirty Years' War, in fact, cavalry had started to perform a series of "auxiliary roles" for the infantry and was rarely used in an autonomous way. During the War of the Austrian Succession (1740-1748), however, some combat episodes showed that the elite heavy cavalry was not as perfect as it may seem. It became apparent, in fact, that it could experience serious problems while operating on broken terrain and when fighting against enemy units that employed "hit-and-run" guerrilla tactics. In particular, the Prussian cuirassiers and dragoons had serious problems in figthing against the efficient light troops deployed by the Austrian Empire: these consisted of semi-regular light cavalrymen, recruited from the inhabitants of Hungary.

The light cavalrymen of the Austrian Army, commonly known as "hussars", had been fighting for decades against the Ottoman Turks on the southern frontier of the Austrian Empire; the latter lived in a state of endless conflict, during which both sides usually launched rapid incursions into the territory of the enemy only to raid and pillage as much as possible. Gradually the Austrian "frontier soldiers" learned how to fight like their enemies, thus becoming experienced in the art of skirmishing and scouting. Their usual area of operations was covered by mountains and woods, where each cavalryman had to move singularly and not in close formation. These fighters were the direct heirs of a glorious military tradition, which had originated in Hungary during the late Renaissance: the hussars, in fact, were the Hungarian national cavalry like the uhlans (lancers) were the Polish national cavalry. Most of the light horsemen from Hungary were farmers during their civil life and lived on the Balkan frontier as "military settlers"; as a result, their innovative tactics derived from direct combat experience and were based on the principle of "open formation". According to the latter, each cavalryman was to advance in an autonomous way but always keeping contact with the other members of his unit; this way he could cover his advance behind the obstacles of the terrain (like a tree, for example) and fire upon the enemy from a favourable position. With this kind of tactics, firearms also became important for cavalry and could start playing a prominent role on the battlefields.

Uniforms of the Russian hussars in 1741, from left to right: trooper of the Hungarian Hussars, trooper of the Moldavian Hussars, officer of the Georgian Hussars, trooper of the Georgian Hussars and trooper of the Serbian Hussars.

During the War of the Austrian Succession, on several occasions, the Hungarian light cavalrymen of the Austrian Army caused serious troubles and losses to Frederick the Great's heavy mounted troops. Initially they were considered as simple "murderers" by the most traditionalist of their enemies, but with the progression of time it became apparent that they could play a very important tactical role. The other great powers of Europe, differently from Austria, could not count on a "militarized border" from which expert light mounted fighters could be recruited; as a result, they started to create their own light cavalry corps by recruiting Balkan mercenaries or prisoners of war. This was the case of France and of several other European nations like Russia, where hussar units proliferated during the central decades of the 18th century. The new light horsemen of the European armies adopted the same uniforms and weapons of the Hungarian hussars, but very soon some "local versions" of the latter started to appear. The general expansion of the light cavalry units continued well after the end of the War of the Austrian Succession, since the combat experiences of the following Seven Years' War (1756-1763) did nothing but confirm the tactical importance of the new light corps. A new form of warfare was born: the "petite guerre" or "little war", which was based on low intensity combat and on hit-and-run tactics.

As previously discussed, Peter the Great tried to raise hussar units inside the Russian Army by recruiting Balkan raiders who were interested in serving as professional soldiers. By 1721, however, this experiment had failed completely, and no hussar units were included into the Russian military forces. In October 1723 Tsar Peter decided to send one of his foreign officers, Jovan Albanez, to recruit some Serbian militiamen in the region of the Habsburg "military border" in the Balkans. Albanez was able to recruit a certain number of volunteers, who were assembled into an irregular corps that was sent to serve in the region of Kiev. In 1727, a few years after Peter the Great's death, the Serbians in Russian service – around 450 men – were formally organized into a light cavalry regiment known as "Serbian Hussars". The latter was progressively enlarged with the absorption of several Ukrainian Cossacks; it served on the border with the Ottoman Empire and was mostly tasked with contrasting the incursions of the Crimean Tatars.

In 1741, as part of his military reforms, Baron Munnich decided to expand the number of hussars in the Russian Army. First, it gave a "regular" status to the existing Serbian Hussars; then, he started recruiting troops for the new light cavalry corps. From 1738 the Russian Army contained a small light cavalry company made up of Georgians coming from the Caucasus, who had left their country as political exiles. The Georgian horsemen distinguished themselves while fighting against the Turks and thus, in 1741, their company was transformed into the new regiment known as "Georgian Hussars". The latter was stationed in Ukraine since 1742, where its members became military settlers and engaged in farming like minor landowners. During 1735-1739 Russia and the Austrian Empire were at war with the Ottomans in the Balkans; this conflict saw a large participation of the Hungarian hussars in Habsburg service, many of whom decided to desert and enter Russian service in exchange for permission to settle in the southern regions of the Russian Empire. In 1741 these former deserters were assembled together to form a new hussar regiment, which became known as "Hungarian Hussars".

The Balkan conflict of 1735-1739 obliged many Orthodox Christians to leave their homes and to search for a new homeland abroad; the Russian authorities welcomed them in the southern regions of Russia, transforming these refugees into military settlers who could serve on the Ukrainian border. Many Moldavians and Wallachians coming from present-day Romania entered Russian service; these all had military experience since they had fought as auxiliaries for the Ottoman Army. In 1741 the Moldavians and Wallachians who had become military settlers were organized as a regular hussar regiment known as "Moldavian Hussars". As a result of the above, by 1742 the Russian Army comprised four regiments of regular light cavalry mostly recruited from Balkan individuals: the Serbian Hussars, the Georgian Hussars, the Hungarian Hussars and the Moldavian Hussars.

Cossacks and Irregular Cavalry

The famous Cossacks have been a fundamental component of the Russian Army for centuries, despite their semi-regular nature; their origins as a specific ethno-social group are still debated today, but the prevailing opinion is that they originated during the 15th century. Starting in this period peasants were leaving their homes in order to become free from the control of their feudal overlords in what was Muscovy, Kiev, Lithuania and Poland; to be serfs in the late medieval period meant having no rights and living in a very harsh way. The former serfs moved to the southern borderlands of these nations, which were not controlled by the aristocrats in a direct way since they were greatly exposed to the raids of warlike nomadic peoples like the Crimean Tatars. Soon after settling along river and trade routes, the former peasants had to organize themselves from a military point of view in order to defend their communities. They started out creating an efficient infantry, then cavalry force while employing traditional weapons like the spear or the sabre. A new "martial people" of runaways was thus born on the borders of south-eastern Europe, who became known as Cossacks.

The latter soon learned that by employing large numbers of firearms they could have a clear tactical advantage over the nomadic peoples, who did not have such modern weapons; as a result, during the 16th century, the Cossacks started to fabricate their own firearms and to use them in a very effective way (they became famous as excellent marksmen). Eventually the term "Cossack" came to describe several groups of people living across several monarchies existing as loyal or independent states as needed. They established trading areas and fortresses/towns; they practiced agriculture and were excellent breeders, but several of them

Officer of the Ukrainian Zaporizhian Cossacks.

became rich thanks to commerce. Initially the Russian authorities perceived the Cossacks as simple brigands; during the 17th century, however, the Russians understood that these people could be of great use in time of war since they could provide excellent light cavalry contingents equipped with firearms. As a result, the Tsars started to hire increasing numbers of Cossacks and used the latter to "colonize" the wild territories of Siberia and of the Caucasus. The Cossacks, guided by capable leaders and working for rich merchants, greatly expanded the national territory of Russia by conquering immense regions that had never been settled before by Europeans. By the end of the 18th century Russia had occupied whole areas of Siberia thanks to the Cossacks and had even established some commercial outposts on the territory of Alaska in North America.

Compared with the other inhabitants of Russia, Cossack communities enjoyed a series of important privileges: they paid no taxes, they paid no trade duties and were permitted to own land despite not being nobles. The Cossack communities were organized into "Hosts" or "Armies", which had both administrative and military functions. Each Host was subdivided into "pulks" or "regiments", which were in turn subdivided into "sotni" or "hundreds". A "sotnia" was a group of settlements capable of providing 100 Cossacks in wartime; as a result, from a military point of view, it could be compared to a company. A regiment could count up to 40 "sotni", but in most cases it had only 5. The fact that the military units corresponded to administrative subdivisions was extremely important, because it created strong personal links between the Cossacks who were part of the same "sotnia". Military life and civil life were strongly related in the Cossack world, since each able-bodied male was a fighter. The richest Cossacks had some servants at their orders, who were runaway peasants living on Cossack lands but not being part of Cossack society; such servants were tasked with looking after remount horses and with transporting the personal objects of their masters on pack-horses.

Artillery and Naval Infantry

Until the outbreak of the Seven Years' War the general organization of the Russian artillery remained more or less the same that had been introduced during the reign of Peter the Great. Since its creation, the artillery was considered to be the most professional and effective branch of service of the Russian Army; its officers were not all aristocrats and underwent selective training before coming to command their units. The Russian artillery always included a certain number of foreign advisors who greatly contributed to its progressive improvement. During the period 1725-1755 the most prominent commanders of the Russian military forces, like Baron Munnich, placed great emphasis on the use of "regimental guns" attached to the various infantry units; this had some negative consequences for the field artillery, since the latter was considered by some as secondary for providing the foot troops with the needed firepower. Hundreds of light field pieces were dispersed among the various infantry regiments, while the "massed" batteries of the field artillery were sometimes too small to play a decisive role during battles.

Following Peter the Great's death in 1725, the naval forces were neglected by the Russian authorities and entered into a period of slow decay. By 1730 the "Regiment of Naval Infantry" had been broken up into a series of independent detachments, each of which was embarked on a different warship of the Russian Navy or was garrisoned in a port and took on the role of "marines".

In addition to the various detachments, there also were a "Battalion of the Admiralty" that acted as the personal guard of the Russian Navy's overall commander and three independent companies tasked with providing the naval infantry detachments to the galleys of the Russian Navy (the latter, like several other European navies, still comprised some vessels having rows in addition to sails).

On 7 June 1733 the Russian naval infantry was completely reorganized, in order to restore its former elite status. Now it was to consist of two marine regiments numbered in progressive order and comprising 12 companies each. The companies of a single regiment were assembled into three battalions with four companies each. A single company mostly consisted of musketeers but also comprised a small number of grenadiers; on campaign or for parades all the grenadiers of a naval infantry regiment – 200 in total – were usually assembled together to form an independent grenadier company. Each of the two marine regiments, like the line infantry ones, had its own artillery section; this was equipped with two 3-pdr guns and four steel mortars. The two regiments of naval infantry were designed to operate on the Baltic Sea; during the 1730s, however, the Russian Navy started to operate a flotilla of small boats on the Don River. This was designed to fight against the Ottomans and needed its own naval infantry detachments. For this reason, in 1734, an independent marine battalion was raised and assigned to the Don Flotilla.

In 1744 the overall structure of the Russian marines was changed again, going back to the one existing in 1730: the two naval infantry regiments were broken up into independent detachments, while the "Battalion of the Admiralty" and the galley companies were re-raised. As a result of the above, a new period of decline began for the Russian naval infantry. This ended only in 1764, when Catherine the Great carried out a general reform of the Russian Navy. Having an efficient marine corps was something extremely important for Russia, since they had to confront several enemies in the Baltic Sea – most notably Sweden – and also deploy naval forces in the Sea of Azov at the mouth of the Don River.

Artillery gunner from the reign of Peter the Great. The red coat with blue facings was distinctive of the artillery.

The Russian Army of Empress Elizabeth, 1741-1762

The Imperial Guard

When Empress Elizabeth ascended to the throne in 1741, she decided to re-constitute the "Cavalier-Guards" as a small detachment with 60 men. The latter escorted the Empress on most occasions and were noted for their loyalty to her. Elizabeth also created another unit inside the Russian Imperial Guard, the so-called "Life-Company". The latter had a quite peculiar history, which began on 25 November 1741 when the grenadiers of the "Preobrazhensky" Regiment - who had supported Elizabeth in the coup that gave her the throne - asked for the privilege of having the Empress as their honorary captain. Elizabeth responded to this request by transforming the grenadier company of the "Preobrazhenskoe" Regiment into an independent corps, which would have acted as her personal foot bodyguard. The new unit assumed the denomination of "Life-Company" and was assigned more or less the same tasks of the mounted "Cavalier-Guards". As a reward to the guardsmen who had supported her, the Empress conferred hereditary nobility on all members of the "Life-Company", something that had never been done before in the Russian Army. The elite foot bodyguard was mostly made up of Elizabeth's intimate friends and assistants. From a formal point of view, the "Cavalier-Guards" were attached to the "Life-Company" and thus there was some strict coordination between the two corps. The latter, with the progression of time, became "parade" units with little combat capabilities; they spent most of the time inside the Imperial Palace and participated to most of the intrigues that took place at court. For this reason, following Empress Elizabeth's death in 1762, they were both disbanded by her successor Peter III.

In addition to the small "Cavalier-Guards", since 1725, the Russian Imperial Guard contained another cavalry unit: the so-called "Life-Regiment". The latter was the heir of the "Life Guard" Cavalry Regiment created by Peter the Great and as such it was a real elite unit with combat capabilities unlike the parade "Cavalier-Guards". The new "Life-Regiment" of 1725 was raised exclusively from the Russian nobility; in 1730 it assumed the official denomination of "Life-Guards" Horse Regiment. All the members of the corps were regarded and paid as officers; command of the unit was given to senior noblemen according to their political abilities more than to their military capabilities. As a result of the above organizational changes, by 1762 the Russian Imperial Guard consisted of six different units: the "Preobrazhensky", the "Semyonovsky", and the "Izmailovsky" regiments, the "Life-Company", the "Life-Guards" Horse Regiment and the "Cavalier-Guards". It should be remembered, in addition, that the "Preobrazhensky" Regiment always continued to comprise one elite company of artillery (the so-called "Bombardier Company") while the other two infantry regiments of the Imperial Guard had one artillery section each.

Grenadier of the "Life-Company", wearing the uniform used during 1742-1762. The fringed "epaulettes" worn on the shoulders as well as the golden piping to coat and waistcoat were distinctive of this small bodyguard corps, which members were all dressed as officers.

The line infantry

Following the accession to the throne of Empress Elizabeth, the general organization of the Russian infantry was modified. A third battalion, having just four companies of musketeers, was added to each of the line infantry regiments. This led to a significant expansion in the ranks of the Russian infantry, in which regiments were stronger than those deployed by most of the contemporary European armies. The standard musketeer company was broken down into four platoons and each platoon consisted of two squads. The musketeer companies of each line infantry regiment were numbered in progressive order – according to seniority – from 1 to 12; the two grenadier companies, instead, had a separate numbering. During 1756-1757, following Russia's entrance into the bloody Seven Years' War, the general structure of the line infantry had to be changed again. Firstly, four new independent regiments of grenadiers were formed by assembling the best elements of the Russian infantry troops together; then the number of battalions making up each line infantry regiment was reduced from three to two.

Only four of the line infantry regiments continued to have three battalions each, preserving a tradition that had been initiated during Peter the Great's reign: the "Moscowsky", the "Kievsky", the "Narvsjy" and the "Ingermlandsky". Each line infantry battalion continued to consist of four musketeer companies and one grenadier company; the formation of the new independent grenadier regiments, in fact, did not lead to the disbandment of the ordinary grenadier companies. The latter, on campaign, were frequently detached from their parent units and assembled together in order to form "temporary" grenadier battalions that were tasked with conducting special operations.

Each regiment of the Russian line infantry had a "senior staff" performing commanding functions and a "junior staff" performing administrative functions. The senior staff consisted of the following elements: one colonel, one lieutenant-colonel, one first-major and one second-major. The junior staff consisted of the following elements: one quartermaster, two adjutants, one auditor, one superintendent, one train officer, one chaplain, one surgeon, two assistant-surgeons, three clerks, three provosts, one drummer and seven oboists. A single musketeer company comprised the following elements: one captain, one lieutenant, two second-lieutenants, two sergeants, one standard-bearer, one armourer, one quartermaster, four corporals, three drummers and 144 privates.

A single grenadier company comprised the following elements: one captain, two lieutenants, three second-lieutenants, four sergeants, one standard-bearer, one armourer, one quartermaster, six corporals, four drummers, two fifers and 200 privates. According to the new organization introduced in 1757, each line infantry regiment was to have a non-combatant "depot battalion" that was employed for recruiting and training new soldiers; this was to consist of four musketeer companies. The four independent regiments of grenadiers were numbered in progressive order and had two battalions each; a single battalion mustered four companies of grenadiers. The senior staff of a grenadier regiment consisted of the following elements: one colonel, one lieutenant-colonel, one

Uniforms of the Russian line infantry in 1756, from left to right: grenadier, musketeer, senior officer and junior officer.

first-major and one second-major; the junior staff was very small and comprised just two officers in addition to some non-combatants. Each grenadier regiment had one depot company in addition to the four active ones; the latter had the following internal composition: one captain, two lieutenants, three second-lieutenants, four sergeants, one standard-bearer, one armourer, one quartermaster, six corporals, four drummers, two fifers and 200 privates.

Since 1757 the artillery section attached to each line infantry regiment was assigned two howitzers in addition to the four light guns that it already had (the number of light guns was later reduced to two). Each artillery section, from a formal point of view, was a detachment provided directly by the Artillery Corps of the Russian Army; it consisted of the following members: one officer, one NCO, five gunners, ten fusiliers and fifteen workers. The fusiliers were tasked with protecting the guns on the battlefield, while the workers were tasked with moving the guns. Each gun was drawn by a two-horse team and the ammunitions of each artillery section were transported into 10 caissons.

During the Seven Years' War, in order to have a highly mobile force that could protect the western border of Russia from the offensives of Frederick the Great, an autonomous "Observation Corps" was created inside the Russian Army. This was not formed by assembling together some of the existing units, but by recruiting new soldiers who had previously been part of the garrison infantry units or of the militia. The Observation Corps consisted of five infantry regiments and one grenadier regiment; it should be noted, however, that since the beginning it had a multi-arms nature because it comprised three artillery detachments and four "hundreds" of Don Cossacks. The first of the three artillery detachments had two companies of field artillery, the second had one company equipped with howitzers, the third had three sections of train. The entire Observation Corps was disbanded at the beginning of 1760, after having failed to perform the duties for which it had been created.

Drummer of the bombardiers wearing the uniform used during 1756-1762. The bombardiers were dressed similarly to the gunners of the field artillery but wore the peculiar grenadier-style headgear shown here. The additional golden lace embroidered on the coat and waistcoat was distinctive of musicians.

Cuirassiers and Dragoons

In 1731, after the formation of the first cuirassier unit, new regulations concerning heavy cavalry drill and tactics were promulgated for the Russian Army. These were based on the contemporary German heavy cavalry doctrine, which prescribed the employment of cuirassiers for conducting frontal charges as well as for firing with their carbines and pistols in front of an advancing enemy. By the outbreak of the Seven Years' War the Russian regulations had become quite old-fashioned, since the heavy cavalrymen of the Prussian Army – for example – no longer dismounted to fire their carbines and were only used to charge. As a result, in 1756, new "updated" regulations were promulgated for the Russian cuirassiers. During that same year another two regiments of cuirassiers were formed, always by converting existing dragoon units, thus bringing the total number of heavy cavalry corps to six. Each cuirassier regiment had a senior staff consisting of one colonel, one lieutenant-colonel, one first-major and one second-major; the junior staff, instead, consisted of the following elements: one quartermaster, one warrant officer, two commissaries, one chief of train, one groom, one chaplain, one surgeon, one assistant-surgeon, two clerks, two assistant-clerks, one kettledrummer, two provosts and six captains. The ten companies included in each regiment were assembled into couples in order to form five squadrons. The internal composition of each single company was this: one lieutenant, one cornet, one sergeant, one quartermaster, one standard-bearer, one armourer, three corporals, two trumpeters, one clerk, one surgeon and 69 troopers.

When the Russian cavalry was completely reorganized in 1756, at the outbreak of the Seven Years' War, the horse grenadiers were re-raised as an independent branch of the Russian mounted troops. The Russian Army needed to have more heavy cavalry units that could fight on equal terms against the Prussian cuirassiers and dragoons; forming new cuirassier regiments, however, would have had enormous costs that the Russian government was in no conditions to sustain. For this reason, it was decided to convert the six best regiments of dragoons into new units of horse grenadiers; these would have been trained very similarly to the cuirassiers but unlike the latter they would have not been equipped with metal cuirasses and would have not been mounted on horses of the Holstein breed. The six new regiments of horse grenadiers had five squadrons each; a single squadron consisted of two companies. In combat the best troopers from each squadron were assembled into a "reserve" half-squadron, which role was that of protecting the flanks and rear of its regiment. The regimental staff of a horse grenadier unit comprised the following elements: one colonel, one lieutenant-colonel, one first-major, one second-major, one quartermaster, one warrant officer, two commissaries, one chief of train, one chaplain, one surgeon, one assistant-surgeon, three clerks, two assistant-clerks, two trumpeters, eight oboists, one kettledrummer and two provosts. A single company had this internal composition: one captain, one first-lieutenant, one second-lieutenant, six NCOs, two drummers and 69 troopers. Like the dragoon regiments, also the horse grenadier ones had a small artillery section attached to their mounted squadrons; this was equipped with two 3-pdr field guns that were operated by six gunners and were transported by six workers.

By 1756 the Russian dragoons consisted of 20 regiments, since two new units had been raised during the previous years. A standard dragoon regiment consisted of five squadrons, each of which comprised two companies. The senior staff of a regiment comprised one colonel, one lieutenant-colonel, one first-major and one second-major. The junior staff, instead, consisted of the following elements: one quartermaster, one warrant officer, two commissaries, two trumpeters, eight oboists, one kettledrummer, one chief of train, one chaplain, one surgeon, one assistant-surgeon, three clerks, two assistant-clerks and two provosts. A single dragoon company mustered the following elements: one captain, one lieutenant, one cornet, eight NCOs, one clerk,

Uniforms of the Russian heavy/medium cavalry in 1756, from left to right: cuirassier, dragoon, officer of the horse grenadiers and trooper of the horse grenadiers.

Uniforms of the Russian foot troops from the late reign of Empress Elizabeth, from left to right: privates of the 1st Pandur Regiment, NCO of the Guard infantry, musketeers of the Guard infantry, officer of the "Life-Company" and private of the 3rd Pandur Regiment.

two drummers, one surgeon and 82 troopers. One of the ten companies making up a regiment was a horse grenadier company; it had the following internal composition: one lieutenant, one sub-lieutenant, one cornet, eight NCOs, one clerk, three drummers, one surgeon and 100 privates. All the dragoon regiments had a small artillery section, which was equipped with two 3-pdr guns. The latter were operated by six gunners and were transported by six workers. In addition to the 20 regiments performing active duties, the Russian Army did comprise also some units of "garrison dragoons". The latter were mostly deployed in the Asian territories, on the border with Persia in the Caucasus or in the vast grasslands of Siberia. The Russian dragoons were still useful as mounted infantry, since they were capable of contrasting the rapid incursions of the nomadic peoples. By 1762 the "garrison dragoons" consisted of seven regiments and two independent squadrons (one of the latter acted as the municipal guard of Moscow).

The Hussars

The expansion of the Russian Army's light cavalry continued also after the outbreak of the Seven Years' War. During the 1750s a fresh wave of Orthodox Christian communities entered the borders of Russia from the Balkans, providing new manpower sufficient to raise another four regiments of hussars: the "Slobodian Hussars" in 1756, the "Macedonian Hussars" in 1759, the "Bulgarian Hussars" in 1759 and the "Yellow Hussars" in 1760. This latter unit, which took its name from the colour of its uniform, was recruited from the Serbian communities that had already settled in Russian Ukraine during the previous decade (which members were known as "New Serbians"). As a result of the above, by 1762 the Russian Army comprised eight regiments of hussars. In addition to the latter active units, it could also count on some garrison corps made up of Balkan military settlers and known as "settled hussars". These were mostly Serbs and lived in the settlement known as "New Serbia", which had been established during 1751 in Russian Ukraine.

In exchange for some land located along the border with Tatar Crimea, the Serbian military settlers were required to form some military units. The latter were tasked with patrolling the frontier but were fully mobilized only in case of war. Each district of New Serbia was to supply one company of hussars as well as one company of light infantry. The hussar companies were 40 in total: 20 were active companies and 20 were reserve companies that could be mobilized in case of need. The 40 companies were assembled into two regiments, known as "1st Hussars of New Serbia" and "2nd Hussars of New Serbia". In 1753, following the example of New Serbia, a new settlement inhabited by Balkan refugees was formed in Russian Ukraine; this was known as "Slavonic Serbia" and was inhabited by Serbians coming from Slavonia. The Russian authorities wanted to use the settlements of New Serbia and Slavonic Serbia as buffer zones between their southern territories and the Ottoman lands by following the model of the Austrian "Grenz" or "Military Border" in the Balkans. As a result, the settlers of Slavonic Serbia were assigned some land in exchange for being required to form some military units. As it happened with New Serbia, the entire male population was registered for military service; the Slavonian refugees were to provide one company of hussars for each of the districts that made up their settlement. Two regiments of Slavonian hussars were thus raised, each having 10 active companies and 10 reserve companies; both units were named after their commanders: "Shevich Hussars" and "Preradovich Hussars".

The Emergence of the Light Infantry

During the first four decades of the 18th century line infantry was the most important component of the European armies, since it made up the bulk of the troops mobilized by the various nations and also because it had acquired a certain tactical superiority over cavalry. Highly trained and well-disciplined, it consisted of musketeers who were able to march and manoeuvre in perfect order by maintaining "shoulder-to-shoulder" close formations. While moving on the battlefield, the line infantrymen advanced in columns; when stopping to open fire upon the enemy, they were deployed into long lines. After some rolling volleys of musketry were exchanged between two opposing infantry formations, a clash could continue in two different ways: on most occasions, one of the two lines was shattered by the enemy fire and thus decided to retreat (usually keeping order among the ranks and re-adopting column formation); on some occasions, instead, it was necessary to fight "hand-to-hand" with bayonets to determine the outcome of the confrontation. Keeping order in the formations and delivering a regular fire were the key factors behind victory; as a result, training was absolutely decisive to transform line infantry into an effective tactical tool.

In most cases battles were extremely static, since maintaining perfect order in the formations obliged the infantrymen to move very slowly. The transition from the column formation to the line one was extremely delicate, since it exposed the infantrymen to the sudden charges of cavalry. When confronting the latter, line infantry usually adopted a standard defensive formation known as "square": this was another kind of "close order", created since long time with the aim of stopping enemy attacks by using the bayonets as "pikes" against mounted troops. The formations and tactics described above were determined by the performances of the muskets that were used during the 18th century; the latter were flintlock weapons, which loading operations were quite complicated. This meant that only one or two balls were shot in a minute, considering the standard performances of a line infantryman with good training. In addition, the flintlock muskets of this period were all smoothbores and thus were extremely inaccurate: when a ball was fired, it came out from the weapon without a precise direction since there were no grooves inside the barrel that could "guide" it.

A flintlock musket was of some use only when fired at 100 or 200 metres from the target; as a result, during a battle, the line infantry formations had to come very close in order to use their weapons with some degree of effectivity. The muskets of this age were also extremely heavy, and this limited a lot the mobility of the foot soldiers; when moving through broken terrain, for example covered with rocks or with trees, it was practically impossible for them to keep the close formations in order. All the main tactical formations had been created for an "ideal" battlefield, consisting of a large plain where the opposing infantries could move without encountering obstacles. In this military system soldiers were not required to think and act in an autonomous way: they only had to move as clockwork toys in order to put in practice the orders received. There was no space for initiative and each infraction of the discipline was immediately punished with very harsh methods. The evolutions required on the battlefield were repeated every day during training sessions, under the incessant beat of the drums.

During the War of the Austrian Succession (1740-1748) some combat episodes showed that the traditional line infantry was not as perfect as it may seem. It became apparent, in fact, that it could experience serious problems while operating on broken terrain and when fighting against enemy units that employed "hit-and-run" guerrilla tactics. The Prussians, in particular, had serious problems in contrasting the efficient light troops deployed by the

Austrian Empire: these consisted of semi-regular light infantrymen, recruited from the warlike inhabitants of the Balkans. The light infantrymen of the Austrian Army had been fighting for decades against the Ottoman Turks on the southern frontier of the Austrian Empire; the latter lived in a state of endless conflict, during which both sides usually launched rapid incursions into the territory of the enemy only to raid and pillage as much as possible. Gradually the Austrian frontier soldiers had learned how to fight like their enemies, thus becoming very expert in the art of skirmishing and scouting. Their usual area of operations was covered with mountains and woods, where each soldier had to move singularly and not in column or line formation.

Most of these frontier soldiers were excellent huntsmen and farmers in their civil lives, living on the Balkan frontier as "military settlers"; as a result, their innovative tactics were derived from hunting and based on the principle of "open formation". Each soldier advanced individually, but keeping contact with the other members of his unit; this way he could cover his advance behind the obstacles of the terrain (like a tree, for example) and fire upon the enemy from a favourable position. On several occasions the Austrian light infantrymen caused serious troubles and losses to Frederick the Great's perfect line infantry. Initially they were considered as simple "murderers" by the most traditionalist of their enemies, but during the course of the War of the Austrian Succession it became apparent that they could play a very important role on the battlefields. The other great powers of Europe, in a different position from Austria, could not count on a "militarized border" from which expert light fighters could be recruited; as a result, they started to create their own light infantry corps from the best hunters and gamekeepers of their communities.

Official portrait of Empress Elizabeth of Russia (ruled 1741-1762). After her death she was suceeded by her nephew Peter from Schleswig-Holstein-Gottorp.

The only exception to this rule was represented by Russia, since the latter could count on the Balkan military farmers living in the settlement of New Serbia. On 24 December 1751 the Russian Army formed its first regiment of Balkan Light Infantrymen or "Pandurs"; this consisted of 20 companies and was soon followed by a second regiment having its same internal composition on 11 January 1752. A few months later, five of the companies in each of the two light infantry regiments were transformed into elite "grenadier companies". The companies of Serbian light infantrymen were quite strong, since each of them mustered around 200 men. In times of peace only 10 companies from each regiment were on active service to patrol the frontier with Tatar Crimea; the other 10 companies were mobilized only in time of war. In 1759 a third regiment of "Pandurs" was raised from the communities of New Serbia; this had to perform only static garrison duties and thus consisted of just four companies (one of which was of grenadiers).

During the Seven Years' War the Russians had to confront the light units deployed by Frederick the Great's Prussian Army. These, the famous "Frei-Corps" or "Free Corps", were mostly recruited from ex-prisoners of war or from foreign deserters; as a result, in most cases, their general quality and discipline were not particularly high. The Frei Corps mostly acted as raiding forces of skirmishers; they were usually organized into "legions" comprising infantry and cavalry as well as some light artillery pieces. Due to their peculiar organizational nature, they could operate as fast-moving and self-contained "miniature armies".

The Frei Corps were frequently employed to conduct special operations but Frederick the Great did not have a very high opinion of them, since their members were prone to indiscipline and desertion. Some historians consider the Frei Corps as the Prussian response to the Balkan light troops in Habsburg service; some

Private of the 1st Pandur Regiment, wearing the uniform used during 1751-1762. The dress is almost identical to that worn by the Balkan light infantrymen in Austrian service. The 2nd Pandur Regiment wore the same uniform as the 1st Pandur Regiment.

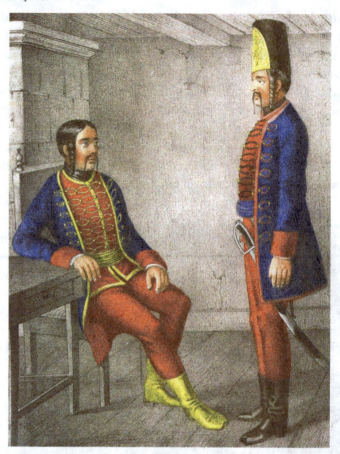

Officer (left) and private (right) of the short-lived 3rd Pandur Regiment

Kalmyk light horseman; the general appearance of this warrior is not very different from that of Gengis Khan's Mongols. ASKB

Nice contemporary picture showing a group of Russian Cossacks during the first half of the 18th century. ASKB

of their units were commanded by competent officers and thus performed quite well; others were extremely short-lived or had a bad conduct in combat. The Russians tried to create their own version of the Frei Corps in 1761, while they were operating against the Prussians in Pomerania. They raised two battalions of "Jägers" or "hunters", i.e. light infantrymen equipped with rifled carbines. These firearms were extremely precise for the standards of the time but needed long time to be re-loaded; as a result, the German-style light infantry of the Jägers was mostly employed to conduct special missions that included sniping and skirmishing from the distance. The two new battalions of light infantry consisted of volunteers and of men provided by the reserve battalions of the line infantry regiments; they also included a certain number of Prussian deserters from the region of Pomerania. Each of the two battalions had five companies of Jägers and one artillery piece; a single company mustered four corporals and 100 privates. The Russian campaign in Pomerania did not last long and thus the Jägers did not have many opportunities to show their valour; they took part to some forest fighting but were disbanded very soon after Russia came out from the Seven Years' War. The two battalions of light infantry raised in 1761 had just been a first "experiment" for the Russian Army; during the following years, in fact, Jägers would have become a permanent component of the Russian military forces.

Cossacks and Irregular Cavalry

By 1755, in addition to the Cossack Hetmanate of Ukraine that was still formally independent from Russia, there were four major Russian Cossack Hosts: Don Cossacks, Volga Cossacks, Yaik Cossacks and Greben Cossacks. The Don Cossacks were the most important and the first to establish some permanent fortified villages as early as 1549. They lived along the banks of the Don River and became official allies of the Russians in 1570 when Tsar Ivan the Terrible recognized them as a political entity. The Don Cossacks were the spearhead of Russia during the latter's conquest of Siberia but also provided large military contingents to the Russian Army; these usually performed very well against "nomad" armies, as well as against enemies who fought in a "conventional" way.

During the 17th century the Don Cossacks fought around the Sea of Azov against the Ottomans, obtaining some great victories; thanks to their efforts, Russia gradually came to control the mouth of the Don River. In 1707 the Don Cossacks refused to deliver fugitive peasants to the Russian authorities, and this led to the outbreak of the so-called "Bulavin Rebellion".[1] Peter the Great crushed the Cossack uprising with brutality in 1708; after these events, the Don Cossack Host lost most of its previous autonomy and had to accept the fact that all its elected leaders had to be confirmed by the Russian government before officially receiving their powers. In 1721 the military forces of the Don Cossacks formally came under the control of the Russian Army; by 1755 they numbered around 16,000 men who were assembled into 22 light cavalry regiments. The Cossack regiments did not have a standard internal structure comparable to that of the Russian regular units; most of them, however, consisted of five companies.

The Volga Cossacks appeared after the establishment of a new Russian defensive line between the Volga River and the Don River; the Russian authorities originally planned to garrison this new defensive line with Don Cossacks, but in 1734 they changed their plans and decided to form the new Volga Cossack Host by detaching the best elements of the Don Cossacks. By 1755 the Volga Cossacks numbered 1,000 men, who were assembled into a single light cavalry regiment.

In 1577, after having obtained control over the course of the Volga River from Kazan to Astrakhan, the Russians sent their troops along the great river in order to disperse the pirates who had infested it for many years. Some of these raiders fled south-east to the Yaik River, which is today known as the Ural River; here they mixed with the local communities of Tatars and formed a new Cossack group known as Yaik Cossacks. Since 1591 they started to be hired by the Russian authorities for border service and for taking part

---
[1] A war fought from 1707 to 1708 between the Don Cossacks under the Ataman Kondraty Bulavin and the Tsarist Army

to expeditions directed to central Asia. By 1755 the Yaik Cossacks numbered around 3,500 men, who were assembled into seven small light cavalry regiments.

The Greben Cossacks, who were part of the Terek Cossack host, settled along the course of the Terek River during the late 16th century and started to collaborate with the Russian authorities during the reign of Peter the Great; they were bitter enemies of the Tatars and their military forces came under Russian control since 1721. Being a small community, by 1755 they numbered just 500 men who made up a single regiment.

In addition to the four Hosts described above there were several minor groups of Cossacks, each of which contributed some military units to the Russian Army: Azov Cossacks, Chuguev Cossacks, Slobodian Cossacks, Khopyor Cossacks, Bakhmut Cossacks, Orenburg Cossacks, Astrakhan Cossacks, Terek Cossacks and Siberian Cossacks. The Azov Cossacks appeared in 1737, when the Russian authorities decided to detach some reliable elements from the Don Cossacks in order to garrison the newly conquered territories located around the Sea of Azov. Possession of those border areas had been contested for long time between the Russians and the Ottomans and thus Russia had to fortify the new frontier in a very effective way. The Azov Cossacks consisted of 500 men, who were assembled into a single infantry regiment that was garrisoned in the important Saint Anna Fortress (located not far from the mouth of the Don).

The Chuguev Cossacks emerged around the half of the 17th century, when a Cossack community was established around the Chuguev Fortress that was located near present-day Kharkiv. Chuguev Fortress was one of the main strongholds defending southern Russia from the incursions of the Ukrainian Cossacks and of the Crimean Tatars; as a result, it had a great military importance. Since 1639 the Chuguev Cossacks collaborated with the Russian authorities, becoming one of the most trusted Cossack groups. In 1740 Baron Munnich tried to transform the Chuguev Cossacks into a regular light cavalry regiment, by giving them a formal military organization and uniforms; the experiment worked but could not be expanded to other Cossack communities. The single regiment made up of Chuguev Cossacks numbered 400 men, who were assembled into three companies; attached to it there were also some Christianized Kalmyks, who were organized as two companies. The Chuguev Cossacks, unlike most of the other minor Cossack groups, participated with distinction to the Russian campaigns of the Seven Years' War.

The Slobodian Cossacks originated from some groups of Orthodox refugees who left the lands of the Polish-Lithuanian Commonwealth to escape religious oppression by the local Catholic authorities. These refugees settled along the Donets River just south of the Russian frontier, soon becoming rivals of the Cossack Hetmanate that occupied a good portion of Ukraine. From 1652 the Slobodian Cossacks started to collaborate with the Russian authorities, performing "border police" duties for the latter. By 1755 they numbered around 5,000 men, who were assembled into a super-large single unit. This was not actually a single regiment, but a "brigade" with five light cavalry regiments; each of the latter included a variable number of half-companies and was equipped with two field guns.

The Khopyor Cossacks emerged after the Bulavin Uprising, when the lands located along the Khopyor River were taken away by the Russians from the rebellious Don Cossacks in order to be re-populated with Don Cossacks who had accepted a Russian amnesty. By 1755 the Khopyor Cossacks mustered just 100 men, who were assembled into a single company.

The Bakhmut Cossacks were created by the Russians in 1748, in order to garrison the strategic Bakhmut Fortress; the latter was located at the junction of the territories inhabited by the Don Cossacks and by the Ukrainian Cossacks of the Cossack Hetmanate. The Bakhmut Cossacks numbered around 300 men in 1755 and thus their small regiment consisted of just three companies, which were tasked with performing static defensive duties.

The Orenburg Cossacks originated from those groups of Cossacks that were settled by the Russians north of present-day Kazakhstan, in order to defend the newly conquered Russian territories of that area from the incursions of the Kazakhs. The Russians founded the important city of Orenburg north of Kazakhstan and fortified it very heavily; the Orenburg Cossacks were created in 1735 exactly to garrison the new urban settlement as well as to colonize the surrounding areas on behalf of the Russian Empire. By 1755 the Orenburg Cossacks numbered around 1,000 men, who were assembled into a single light cavalry regiment. The latter saw much action against the Kazakhs and thus was a very battle-hardened unit.

The Astrakhan Cossacks were formed in 1737, when the Russian government relocated a certain number of Volga Cossacks to the region of Astrakhan; these were organized into a small regiment with three companies, which were mostly tasked with escorting couriers and with patrolling the frontier. With the progression of time the regiment was expanded, to the point that in 1755 it mustered five companies.

The Terek Cossacks were the most important Cossack community living on the Caucasus; they first appeared around 1520, when the Russians started colonizing the banks of the Terek River. The early Terek Cossacks consisted of Caucasian refugees who decided to flee from their homeland after having been defeated by the Russians and who moved southwards. The newcomers, after reaching the Terek River, mixed with the local populations and in particular with the Ossetians. The new Terek Cossacks fought several campaigns against the Ottomans in Georgia. In 1720, as the result of a gradual process, they became part of the Russian military forces and thus started to participate to the expeditions organized by Russia against Persia. By 1755 the Terek Cossacks numbered around 500 men, who were assembled into a single regiment; attached to this there was a semi-autonomous squadron made up of Armenians and Georgians.

The Siberian Cossacks were the heirs of those Don Cossacks who, under the guidance of Yermak Timofeyevich, conquered a large portion of Siberia during the years 1582-1585. They were settled to the east from the Orenburg Cossacks and were mostly tasked with garrisoning a chain of small wooden forts that were called "ostrogs". The latter protected the Russian trade routes crossing Siberia, which were of fundamental importance for the fur trade that had been established by the Russian merchants of the Stroganov family at the end of the 16th century. By 1755 the Siberian Cossacks did not yet have a formal military organization.

The irregular light cavalry of the Russian Army not only consisted of Cossacks, since it included some auxiliary contingents provided by the nomadic peoples of the steppes living on the borders of the Russian Empire: Bashkirs, Tatars, Mesheryaks and Kalmyks. The Bashkirs lived between Siberia and Kazakhstan, not far from the Russian outpost of Orenburg; they fought as mounted archers equipped with powerful composite bows and wearing cuirasses of chainmail. In case of need, they could provide 6,000 horsemen to their Russian allies; during the Seven Years' War, 500 of the latter fought in Germany, terrorizing the local civilians. The Tatars lived around the urban settlements of Kazan and had been soundly defeated by Tsar Ivan the Terrible before becoming allies of the Russians. They had many features in common with the Bashkirs and – if required to do so – could mobilize 20,000 light horsemen for the Russian Army.

The Mesheryaks lived on a relatively small area located between the territories of the Bashkirs and those of the Tatars. They were enemies of the Bashkirs and thus formed a strong alliance with the Russians before the other nomadic peoples. The Kalmyks lived along the banks of the Volga River and – together with the Bashkirs – were considered to be the most effective nomadic fighters on whom the Russians could count. They could mobilize around 40,000 tribal warriors, 500 of whom participated to the Seven Years' War. The Russian Army also comprised a single regiment of "Christianized Kalmyks", which numbered around 800 men and was extremely loyal to the Russian authorities.

Most of the Cossack units, like the irregular cavalry contingents provided by the nomadic peoples, were famous as violent plunderers and thus were extremely precious as foragers for the Russian Army. They conducted scouting missions to gather intelligence about the enemy and were real masters in organizing ambushes; each Cossack had two horses and thus could travel for long distances without pauses. The Russian irregular cavalry was also very useful for routing a defeated enemy or for surrounding isolated enemy detachments. What the Cossacks lacked most was discipline, since on several occasions it was almost impossible for their Russian officers to control them: they were not paid for their military services and thus the only sources of income that they had derived from plundering. Sometimes the presence of Cossacks during a campaign was used as a "psychological weapon" by the Russians, since the civilians of eastern Europe were terrorized by the irregular cavalrymen in Russian service.

The Reform of the Artillery and the Technical Corps

In 1755 Count Peter Ivanovich Shuvalov was asked by the Russian government to reorganize the artillery along modern lines, improving its standards of service and introducing new pieces of equipment. Shuvalov re-structured the Russian artillery on two main units: the "Field Artillery Regiment" and the "Regimental Artillery Regiment". The first was designed to provide massed batteries during field battles, while the second provided the artillery sections to the various infantry regiments. Both corps, which were numbered in progressive order, were more administrative units than combat ones since their components usually served in an autonomous way. The Field Artillery Regiment was not created by Count Shuvalov, because it existed since the reign of Peter the Great. According to the reorganization of 1756 it was to consist of two battalions having five companies each: one company of bombardiers and four companies of gunners. A standard bombardier company consisted of the following elements: four officers, eleven NCOs, four musicians, 45 bombardiers and 135 auxiliary workers.

Gunner of the field artillery wearing the uniform used during 1756-1762. Since its foundation by Peter the Great, the Russian artillery had been dressed in red.

A standard gunner company consisted of the following elements: four officers, eight NCOs, two drummers, 40 gunners and 80 fusiliers tasked with protecting artillery pieces on the battlefield. Each company acted as a battery on the field; the gunner companies were equipped with field guns, while the bombardier companies operated mortars and howitzers. As a result of the above, the bombardiers played a very important role during siege operations and thus were considered to be the "elite" of the Russian artillery. The Regimental Artillery Regiment was created by Count Shuvalov by assembling together, at least from an administrative point of view, all the artillery sections attached to the infantry units. It was to consist of two battalions with five companies each, four of gunners and one of bombardiers; this internal structure, however, existed only on paper since the ten companies/batteries of the regiment were fractioned into over 50 small detachments that were attached to the infantry regiments as well as to the dragoon regiments. The field pieces employed by the Field Artillery Regiment were standard 6-pdrs, 8-pdrs and 12-pdrs which were quite similar to those deployed by the contemporary European armies; they were made of brass and did not have a standard design for carriages. Each field gun was accompanied by two small ammunition wagons carrying 120 rounds of ball and 30 rounds of canister. Until 1758 the bombardier companies of the Russian Army operated mortars of different calibres, but these were all progressively replaced by much more modern howitzers.

Unlike the artillery of other European armies, the Russian one included a variety of unusual or experimental guns in its equipment; these comprised the so-called "secret howitzer" designed by Count Shuvalov during his artillery reform, which had an oval rather than a round bore. This 18-calibre howitzer was known as "secret" because nobody in the Russian Army was allowed to see its innovative muzzle, which was shielded by a copper lid that was fastened by a lock. If anyone disclosed information about this gun they were subject to the death penalty. The "secret howitzer" was designed to act like a shotgun on the battlefield, spraying a flat swathe of canister rounds parallel to the ground. Reloading it was a quite complex operation, since it fired a tin canister containing 168 musket balls.

The Russian "secret howitzer" was a quite spectacular weapon for the standards of the time since it could potentially kill an entire infantry company with a single round. In 1756, in order to operate the new artillery weapon that he had designed, Shuvalov organized an autonomous "Secret Howitzer Corps". This initially consisted of three companies/batteries, which were soon increased to four. Each of the bombardier companies that made up the unit comprised the following elements: four officers, ten NCOs, four musicians, 23 bombardiers and 140 auxiliary workers. In the early months of 1758, a fifth company was added to the existing ones and the internal composition of the bombardier companies became as follows: seven officers, fourteen NCOs, three musicians, 28 bombardiers, 14 gunners, 164 fusiliers and 112 auxiliary workers. The gunners were added because each company/battery of the corps started to have seven "unicorn" guns in addition to 14 "secret howitzers".

Uniforms of the Russian artillery in 1756, from left to right: officer of the bombardiers, drummer of the bombardiers, gunner and fusilier.

The "unicorn" was another innovative artillery weapon developed during Shuvalov's reform of the Russian artillery. It was 10-calibre long and had a conical breech; it could be considered a cross between a cannon, a howitzer and a mortar. Although it carried the same range of canister shot used by the "secret howitzer", it was capable of firing ball and was quite quick to reload. Being light and easy to manoeuvre, the "unicorn" was produced in two different versions: one with a shorter barrel that was assigned to some of the infantry's artillery sections and one with a longer barrel that was assigned to the Secret Howitzer Corps. According to Shuvalov's plans the "unicorn" would have become the new standard weapon of the infantry's artillery sections, but this did not happen since the standard 3-pdr guns of the infantry regiments were never completely replaced. The versatility of the "unicorn", however, permitted the formation of the first "experimental" units of horse artillery of the Russian Army; since 1758, in fact, some temporary mounted artillery batteries equipped with four "unicorns" each were created. These, being attached to the major cavalry units, were quite short-lived and were all disbanded by the end of Russia's participation to the Seven Years' War.

In 1758 the Secret Howitzer Corps was re-named "Bombardier Corps"; a few months later, in 1759, it received the new official denomination of "3rd Regiment of Artillery" and thus started to have a permanent nature. As we anticipated above, during the Seven Years' War - in order to have a highly-mobile force that could protect the western border of Russia from the offensives of Frederick the Great - an autonomous "Observation Corps" was created inside the Russian Army. When the latter was disbanded in the early months of 1760, its infantry soldiers were used to create some new units of "fusiliers" tasked with protecting the batteries of the artillery.

In the Russian Army, like in many contemporary European armies, the term "fusilier" was employed to designate some infantrymen who were assigned to the escort of the artillery. Two regiments of fusiliers were created inside the Russian Army in 1760, each of them consisting of nine companies. These were supplemented by a small corps known as "Fusilier Reserve" and consisting of just three companies. After the end of the hostilities the two Fusilier Regiments were retained in service, while the Fusilier Reserve was disbanded. By the time of the Seven Years' War the artillery pieces of the Russian Army were still transported by civilian contractors, who were quite unreliable since they did not have to respect military discipline and usually abandoned the field when some enemy forces came too close to them. In order to replace the civilian contractors with proper soldiers, in 1757 it was decided to organize an artillery train inside the Russian Army. This consisted of 600 men assembled into three companies, which were tasked with moving field guns during campaigns; the new corps, however, did not play any active role during the hostilities and thus was soon disbanded. The artillery of the Russian Army did not comprise only the "active" units described above, but also some garrison corps that were scattered across the fortifications of the Russian Empire. By 1755 the "garrison artillery" mustered around 6,000 gunners, who were assembled into many independent companies and detachments.

In addition to the artillery, the Russian Army also comprised other technical corps that performed important auxiliary duties: the Engineer Regiment and the Pontoon Company. The first to understand that the Russian Army needed to have some expert engineer officers in its ranks was Peter the Great, who created the first military school for the instruction of engineer officers as early as 1712. Ten years later, in 1722, 275 men were raised to act as the "labour force" of the new Engineer Corps; the latter, by 1755, consisted of three companies and had been organized as a proper unit known as "Engineer Regiment".

The Russian engineer officers were of excellent quality, since they underwent some effective training and were instructed by competent foreign experts. The three companies placed under their orders had different specializations: one was of miners, one was of pioneers and one was of sappers. By 1755 each of the companies had 50 engineer officers and 250 privates. The Engineer Regiment was mostly tasked with building field fortifications during campaigns; as a result, when needed, it could be supplemented with some companies detached from the infantry regiments. In practice the Engineer Regiment formed the "trained core" that supervised the operations of the whole army when field engineering was required. In addition to those who were part of the Engineer Regiment, the Russian Army of 1755 did comprise also 600 engineer officers who were scattered across the Russian Empire; these "garrison engineers" served in the major fortresses of their country and were tasked with supervising the maintenance of the latter.

The Pontoon Company was a small independent unit that obtained its manpower from the Russian Navy and not from the Russian Army; it could supply 90 pontoons in time of war and was responsible for the construction of timber bridges. As a result of the above it was an essential component of the Russian Army, considering how many large rivers crossed the lands of eastern Europe. The Pontoon Company was commanded by a naval lieutenant and consisted of just 56 men; the latter included boatswains for carpentry and armourers for blacksmithing. Since 1759 it was re-equipped with collapsible canvas pontoons, something that greatly improved its general mobility.

The Holstein Army of Peter III, 1762

A Short and Turbulent Reign

On 5 January 1762 Empress Elizabeth of Russia died. With no direct heirs, she had groomed her nephew Peter who was the son of Charles Frederick of Holstein-Gottorp and Anna Petrovna (a younger sister of Empress Elizabeth) as the new Tsar. The marriage between Charles Frederick and Anna had been the result of some careful political calculations, since the German Duchy of Holstein-Gottorp had a very significant strategical importance for the Russian Empire. Holstein-Gottorp was located on the Baltic Sea and was a tributary state of the Kingdom of Denmark; for long time, however, the rulers of the duchy had tried to win their independence from Denmark by establish a dynastic alliance with the Kingdom of Sweden. The same Charles Frederick was a nephew of Charles XII of Sweden and thus had a strong anti-Danish attitude in foreign policy.

After the Great Northern War, following the defeat of Sweden, the Duchy of Holstein-Gottorp came under an increasing Russian political influence that led to the marriage between Charles Frederick and Peter the Great's younger daughter Anna Petrovna. Peter, the child who was born from this union in 1728, became Duke of Holstein-Gottorp as early as 1739 due to the sudden death of his father. After spending his early years in Germany where he became an admirer of Frederick the Great, he moved to Russia where he was chosen as heir by his aunt Empress Elizabeth and converted to Orthodoxy. Elizabeth favoured Peter in every possible way and even organized his marriage with a German princess, Sophia Augusta Frederica of Anhalt-Zerbst (the future Catherine the Great). Sophia moved to Russia and took the name of Ekaterina (Catherine) after converting to Orthodoxy. The marriage between Peter – who had been made Grand Duke of Russia by Empress Elizabeth – and Catherine took place in 1745.

Peter became Tsar in 1762 with the name of Peter III; from the beginning of his reign, he started to act very differently from Empress Elizabeth who had preceded him. First, he decided to withdraw the Russian Army from the ongoing Seven Years' War. The new Tsar had a personal veneration for the Prussian monarch Frederick the Great, whom he considered to be a military genius and an example to follow. As a result, he could not accept that his country was at war

Official portrait of Tsar Peter III, who ruled for a few months during 1762.

with the man he admired most. Peter III's decision to make peace with Prussia was unexplainable to most of the Russian government's members: before the ascendancy of the new Tsar, in fact, the Russian Army had obtained a series of important victories over the Prussians. The latter were completely exhausted and no longer had the resources needed to defend their homeland from renewed Russian attacks. The peace treaty that Peter III signed with Frederick the Great, in addition, was extremely favourable to Prussia: the Russians gave up all the territories that they had conquered in Prussia and were to provide a contingent of 12,000 soldiers to Frederick the Great. Russia switched from being an enemy of Prussia to an ally; this had significant political and military consequences for the ongoing conflict, since Frederick the Great could recapture the crucial region of Silesia from his Austrian allies and force the latter to the negotiating table.

Peter III was never particularly interested in the destiny of his Russian realm, since he always preferred to act as the Duke of Holstein-Gottorp and not as the Tsar of Russia. He disliked Russian culture and considered himself as a German monarch. Soon after making peace with Prussia, he started gathering a Russian expeditionary force in northern Pomerania, with the objective of invading the Kingdom of Denmark. His main political ambition, in fact, was that of expanding the Duchy of Holstein-Gottorp as much as possible. The war that Peter III was preparing against Denmark was considered as "unpatriotic" by the Russians, who would have preferred to continue the struggle against Frederick the Great. The new Tsar was soon hated by most of his subjects due to his "unorthodox" moves of foreign policy. In addition, the nobility began to turn against him, for passing a series of reforms that were aimed at cancelling the Russian aristocracy's traditional monopoly on trade.

The Holstein Army

Knowing very well that he was hated by the Imperial Guard and by the rest of the Russian Army, Peter III decided to transfer a large portion of the Holstein Army to Russia in order to count on the military support of his reliable German soldiers in case of palace coups or internal rebellions. Before the outbreak of the Great Northern War, the Holstein Army was very small and consisted of the following units:

- Drabant Guard (a squadron of mounted bodyguards);
- Four regiments of infantry (one being classified as "Foot Guards");
- Two regiments of dragoons (one being classified as "Horse Guards");
- One artillery company (garrisoned in the fortress of Tönning).

In 1700 the ruling Duke of Holstein-Gottorp hoped to remain neutral during the new conflict that had just started between Sweden and Denmark; the independence of his small state, after all, was guaranteed by an international convention that put Holstein-Gottorp under the military protection of Sweden and of the "Maritime Powers" (i.e. the British and Dutch naval squadrons). During the years following the Peace of Travendal, which was signed in 1700 and temporarily ended the hostilities between Sweden and Denmark, the Holstein Army was enlarged with the creation of two new units: an infantry regiment (having "guard" status and being entirely made up of Swedish personnel) and a heavy cavalry regiment. Another company of artillery was also raised during this period. During those same years, the ruling Duke of Holstein-Gottorp married the sister of Charles XII (thus becoming one of the possible future candidates to the Swedish throne).

The regiments of Holstein infantry were structured similarly to the contemporary Swedish ones, with eight musketeer companies assembled into two battalions plus one grenadier company attached to the first battalion. The original regiment of Foot Guards had two companies of grenadiers, one for each battalion. The cavalry units had four squadrons with two companies each. In 1714, according to a convention signed between Holstein-Gottorp and Sweden, the following units from the ducal army passed into Swedish service: the "Foot Guards" regiment, one infantry regiment, the "Horse Guards" regiment and the heavy cavalry regiment. With the end of the Great Northern War the Duchy of Holstein-Gottorp, Sweden's only proper ally during the conflict, had to cede a large part of its territories to Denmark; despite this, under Duke Charles Frederick's rule (1721-1739), the Holstein Army was re-built almost from zero and significantly expanded.

When Peter became Duke of Holstein-Gottorp his military forces consisted of the following units: one battalion of grenadiers, three regiments of musketeers, one cuirassier regiment, one dragoon regiment, one artillery battalion and one invalid corps. In 1758 a new infantry unit was raised specifically for garrisoning the fortress of Tönning and in 1760 the Holstein cavalry was expanded with the addition of a new hussar regiment. Shortly before becoming Tsar, Peter completely reorganized his Holstein military forces and raised several new units. By 1762 this was the composition of the Holstein Army:

- "Manteuffel" Musketeer Regiment.
- "Prince William" Musketeer Regiment.
- "Prince August" Musketeer Regiment.
- "Kettenburg" Musketeer Regiment.
- "Essen" Grenadier Battalion.
- "Weiss" Grenadier Battalion.
- "Kruger" Garrison Regiment.
- "Life-Cuirassiers" Regiment;
- "Leuven" Cuirassier Regiment.
- "Lotcova" Cuirassier Regiment.
- "Life-Dragoons" Regiment.
- "Prince George Ludwig" Dragoon Regiment.
- "Life-Hussars" Regiment.
- "Zobeltis" Hussar Regiment.
- Artillery Battalion.

All the units listed above were transferred to Russia or sent detachments to Russia in order to support Peter on his new throne. The internal organization of the Holstein military corps was modelled on that of the contemporary Prussian ones. The four regiments of musketeers had two battalions each; a single battalion mustered five companies of musketeers and one company of grenadiers. The two elite grenadier battalions had six grenadier companies each, while the single "garrison regiment" consisted of two battalions with six companies each plus two companies of invalids. The heavy cavalry regiments of cuirassiers and dragoons had five squadrons with two companies each, while the two hussar regiments had a larger internal establishment with eight squadrons having two companies each. One squadron of each dragoon regiment was made up of horse grenadiers. The Artillery Battalion had six companies/batteries, each of which included a certain number of fusiliers tasked with protecting the gunners. Peter III transformed the whole Holstein Army into his own personal "Imperial Guard" after becoming Tsar of Russia, something that caused great discontent among his new subjects and the military. The Russian units of the Imperial Guard, which had been greatly favoured during the reign of Empress Elizabeth, could not accept the fact that now a large expeditionary force made up of foreign soldiers was garrisoned not far from their barracks. The Holstein military forces were quite numerous and thus could potentially crush any coup organized by the Russian court against Peter III; they consisted of experienced and professional German soldiers, who disliked the Russians and who wanted to assume a prominent role inside the Russian Army.

Grenadier of the "Izmailovsky" Regiment wearing the short-lived "German uniform" introduced by Peter III in 1762. This had frontal lapels, decorative embroidery on the buttonholes and golden cords on the right shoulder. The "mitre" cap is in perfect Prussian style.

The new Tsar considered the Russian units of the Imperial Guard as a strong menace for his personal power and thus intervened on their internal organization with the objective of weakening them. First of all, he ordered the disbandment of both the "Life-Company" and the "Cavalier-Guards"; the latter, in fact, served very near

(Left) The uniforms worn by the grenadiers of the Holstein Army's infantry, from left to right: private of the "Essen" Grenadier Battalion, officer of the "Weiss" Grenadier Battalion, private of the "Weiss" Grenadier Battalion, grenadier of the "Kettenburg" Musketeer Regiment, grenadier of the "Manteuffel" Musketeer Regiment, grenadier of the "Prince William" Musketeer Regiment, musketeer of the "Prince William" Musketeer Regiment and grenadier of the "Prince August" Musketeer Regiment.

Holstein officer of the "Manteuffel" Musketeer Regiment.

Holstein grenadier private (left) and grenadier officer (right) of the "Prince William" Musketeer Regiment.

Holstein musketeer officer (left) and musketeer private (right) of the "Kettenburg" Musketeer Regiment.

to his person and thus could potentially organize his assassination. Peter III also tried to reduce the combat capabilities of the Imperial Guard's major units. The "Preobrazhensky" Regiment was re-structured on one battalion of grenadiers and two battalions of musketeers; the first had six companies of grenadiers, while the second had one company of grenadiers and five companies of musketeers. The Bombardier Company attached to the regiment was detached from its parent unit and was assembled together with the artillery detachments of the other two infantry regiments of the Imperial Guard in order to form an autonomous "Bombardier Battalion" having two companies. Both the "Semyonovsky" Regiment and the "Izmailovsky" Regiment were re-structured on two musketeer battalions, each of which had one company of grenadiers and five companies of musketeers. Peter III also modified the organization of the elite independent units of grenadiers that existed in the Russian line infantry, by re-structuring the four existing regiments as six autonomous battalions. This change was made according to the contemporary German practice of organizing grenadier units as independent battalions and not as regiments. All the modifications described above were perceived as something very hostile by the members of the Russian Imperial Guard, who soon started to plan the removal of Peter III; in doing this they found a precious ally in the Tsar's wife, the ambitious Catherine.

(Left) Uniforms of the Holstein heavy and medium cavalry units, from left to right: officer of the "Life-Cuirassiers" Regiment, horse grenadier of the "Prince George Ludwig" Dragoon Regiment, horse grenadier officer of the "Life-Dragoons" Regiment and cuirassier of the "Lotcova" Cuirassier Regiment.

(Right) Holstein NCO (left) and trooper (right) of the "Life-Cuirassiers" Regiment.

(Top left) Uniforms of the Holstein "Prince August" Musketeer Regiment, from left to right: grenadier, musketeer, grenadier officer and musketeer. As clear from this picture, the uniforms of the Holstein Army's infantry were greatly influenced by the contemporary Prussian military fashion.

(Top right) Holstein private (left) and officer (right) of the "Weiss" Grenadier Battalion.

(Right) Holstein private of the "Kruger" Garrison Regiment.

Holstein troopers of the "Leuven" Cuirassier Regiment.

Holstein trooper (left) and officer (right) of the "Lotcova" Cuirassier Regiment.

Holstein trooper of the "Life-Dragoons" Regiment.

Holstein horse grenadier trooper (left) and horse grenadier officer (right) of the "Prince George Ludwig" Dragoon Regiment.

Holstein officers of the "Zobeltis" Hussar Regiment (left) and of the "Life-Hussars" Regiment (right). The uniforms shown here are almost identical to those of the contemporary Prussian hussars.

Holstein gunner (left) and NCO (right) of the Artillery Battalion. The grenadier-style cap shown here was worn by most of the European "fusilier" units that were tasked with escorting the artillery.

The Russian Army of Catherine the Great, 1762-1796

The Removal of Peter III

Catherine was the daughter of a minor German ruler – the Prince of Anhalt-Zerbst – and of a female member of the noble family that ruled Holstein-Gottorp; as a result, she was related to her future husband Peter III. Catherine's marriage with the Grand Duke of Russia was not a happy one from the beginning, mostly because of Peter's vicious temperament and of Catherine's dislike of the latter.

Once in Russia, however, the former German princess spared no effort to ingratiate herself not only with Empress Elizabeth but also with the Russian people. She applied herself to learning Russian language with zeal and tried to learn all the most important traditions that were part of Russian culture. It appears that Catherine soon came to love her new country, building up a special relationship with the Russian people; she was admired for her beauty and for her intelligence, while her husband Peter was disliked by most of the population. With the progression of time Catherine's popularity became very significant, especially after she started to support the circles of the Russian court that opposed Peter's ascendancy to the throne. Catherine had liaisons with several important members of the Russian aristocracy, and it has been proposed that from 1749 she started planning a coup against her husband. After becoming Empress Consort in 1762, Catherine tried to limit the eccentricities and new policies of her husband in every possible way; she had already established stable relations with the most prominent members of her court and thus could easily remove Peter III from the throne if the right opportunity came.

In July 1762, just six months after becoming Tsar, Peter III abandoned the court at Saint Petersburg and moved to a nearby palace with his Holstein-born courtiers and relatives. He was naturally followed by his Holstein military units, which established their main base at Oranienbaum where Peter's new "German court" was located. Catherine remained in Saint Petersburg and decided to act very rapidly in order to remove her husband from the throne. She visited the barracks of the "Izmailovsky" Regiment and delivered a speech to the soldiers of the "Semyonovsky" Regiment, asking for the support of the Imperial Guard. Through her relationships with powerful military men of the court - Grigori Orlov and Grigori Potemkin - she had developed a strong relationship with the guards. She informed the guardsmen that her husband was a menace for the stability of Russia and that she was ready to rule on her own, having as main objective that of guaranteeing peace and prosperity to her Russian subjects.

The Imperial Guard responded with great enthusiasm to Catherine's "call to arms", also because it was invited to do so by the important courtiers who were collaborating with Catherine for the success of the military coup. The Orthodox clergy supported Catherine as well as the inhabitants of Saint Petersburg, who armed themselves to help the Imperial Guard in case the Holstein military forces would have marched on the Russian capital. In a few hours, without having the time for organizing an effective reaction, Peter III was informed at Oranienbaum that both the Russian Army and the Russian Navy had pronounced themselves in favour of Catherine. Before he could order to his troops to march against the rebels, he was arrested by some soldiers of the Russian Imperial Guard and was forced to abdicate on 9 July 1762. He was then transported to Ropsha as a prisoner, where he died after just eight days of captivity. Peter III's death is still surrounded by mystery, but it is highly probable that he was killed by one of Catherine's court favourites who had participated to the successful military coup. Catherine was crowned Empress of Russia in Moscow on 22 September 1762; this event marked the beginning of a new phase in the history of Russia and of Eastern Europe.

One of the new Empress' first acts was to restore the organization of the Imperial Guard that existed before the ascendancy of Peter III; the "Life-Company" and the "Cavalier-Guards" were re-raised, while the "Preobrazhensky" Regiment was brought back to its usual extra-large establishment with four battalions (each consisting of one grenadier company and four musketeer companies) plus the Bombardier Company. The Bombardier Battalion created by Peter III was disbanded; both the "Semyonovsky" Regiment and the "Izmailovsky" Regiment were brought back to their usual establishment with three battalions (having one grenadier company and four musketeer companies each) plus an artillery detachment. The grenadier units of the Russian line infantry went back to their previous organization with four regiments.

The Holstein military units that had served Peter III with great loyalty and which had been temporarily attached to the Russian Army were disarmed and sent back home. After having been informed of Catherine's coup, the Holstein military officers had invited Peter III to transform Oranienbaum into a fortified stronghold in order to attempt a resistance. Initially the Tsar seemed to be favourable to this option, but after learning that his German troops did not have enough ammunition and supplies to resist a long siege, he decided that there was no sense in causing the death of his Holstein soldiers. Oranienbaum was soon surrounded by the Russian Imperial Guard after Peter's arrest and no incidents occurred during the disarming of the 3,500 Holstein troops. A few of the Holsteiners decided to remain in Russia and swore an oath of allegiance to the new regime, while the majority were embarked on Russian ships and went back to Holstein. The convoy was almost entirely destroyed by a violent storm during the journey and thus the "adventure" of the Holstein soldiers in Russia had a very unlucky final.

The Imperial Guard and the Gatchina Troops

During the long reign of Empress Catherine, the Imperial Guard was expanded with the formation of several new units that had a quite innovative character. The line infantry always continued to consist of three major units: "Preobrazhensky" Regiment, "Semyonovsky" Regiment and "Izmailovsky" Regiment. The first had an extra-large establishment with four battalions (each consisting of one grenadier company and four musketeer companies), while the other two had three battalions each (with one grenadier company and four musketeer companies). Attached to the "Preobrazhensky" Regiment there was the elite Bombardier Company of artillery, while the other two units had standard artillery sections. The small bodyguard corps of the Life Company and of the Cavalier Guards were retained in service and continued to perform their ceremonial duties; also the "Life Guards" Horse Regiment did not see any alteration in its internal organization, since it continued to consist of five squadrons with two companies each like all the heavy cavalry units of Russian Army.

On 19 February 1775 it was decided to create a corps of hussars inside the Imperial Guard, by assembling together the best elements of the existing "line" hussar units. The new corps initially consisted of just a single squadron, known as "Life Hussar Squadron"; in 1796, shortly after Empress Catherine's death, a second squadron of hussars was added to the first one. On 20 April 1775, as a reward for the loyalty of her Cossacks, Catherine decided to include a new Cossack corps inside the Imperial Guard. This initially consisted of a single squadron, which was recruited from the most trusted elements of the Don Cossacks and of the Chuguev Cossacks. Each of the latter had its own detachment inside the unit. The new light cavalry squadron was tasked with guarding the personal convoy of Catherine when the latter moved across the Russian Empire.

Trooper of the "Cavalier-Guards", wearing the uniform used during 1764-1796 for "normal" occasions. Note the rich decorative embroiderings of this dress.

Trooper of the "Life-Guards" Horse Regiment, wearing the uniform used during 1742-1762.

In 1796 a second squadron of Cossacks was added to the existing one. Shortly after Catherine the Great's death, his son and successor Tsar Paul I decided to assemble together the two squadrons of hussars and the two squadrons of Cossacks existing in the Imperial Guard as a single light cavalry regiment. The existence of this "mixed" corps (half-hussar and half-Cossack), however, did not last for long since already in 1798 both the Life-Hussars and the Life-Cossacks were re-organized as independent regiments of the Russian Imperial Guard. During the Seven Years' War, as we have already seen, the "Jäger" light infantry deployed by several armies demonstrated to have excellent combat capabilities; being armed with rifled carbines and being recruited from individuals who were excellent marksmen in their civil life (like huntsmen or gamekeepers), it rapidly became an important component of some major armies like the Prussian one. Following the example of the latter, the Russians created their own corps of Jägers not only inside the line infantry but also inside the Imperial Guard.

In 1770 one company of Jägers was attached to each of the three infantry regiments included into the Imperial Guard; the three small corps of light infantry, equipped with rifled carbines, performed quite well and thus soon became permanent. On 9 November 1796 Tsar Paul I decided to detach the three jager companies from their parent regiments and to use them to raise an independent light infantry corps inside his Imperial Guard. This assumed the official denomination of "Life-Guards Jager Battalion" and was structured on three companies. Always on 9 November 1796, the new Russian monarch ordered the creation of an artillery unit inside his Imperial Guard; this was formed by assembling together the Bombardier Company of the "Preobrazhensky" Regiment with the artillery sections of the other two infantry regiments. The new corps was given the official denomination of "Life Guards Artillery Battalion" and consisted of three infantrycompanies/batteries. As clear from the above, by 1796 the Russian Imperial Guard had become a real "miniature army" comprising light units of infantry and cavalry in addition to some artillery; a lot had changed in its internal structure since the days of Peter the Great.

Empress Catherine's son and heir, Paul, showed a great interest in military matters since his childhood and developed a real fascination for Frederick the Great of Prussia exactly like Tsar Peter III. His main ambition was to transform the Russian Army into an exact copy of the Prussian one; to achieve this objective, following the example of his ancestor Peter the Great, he decided to create an experimental "miniature army" that would have been

The uniforms worn by the jager companies of the Imperial Guard's infantry during 1786-1796, from left to right: "Preobrazhenskoe" Regiment, "Semyonovskoe" Regiment and "Izmailovsky" Regiment. Each company had a different kind of headgear.

Grenadiers of the "Preobrazhenskoe" Regiment (left), "Semyonovskoe" Regiment (centre) and "Izmailovsky" Regiment (right) wearing the uniform used during 1763-1786.

Musketeer of the "Preobrazhenskoe" Regiment (left), musketeer of the "Semyonovskoe" Regiment (centre) and musketeer NCO of the "Izmailovsky" Regiment (right) wearing the uniform used during 1763-1786.

Officer of the Imperial Guard's infantry (left), musketeer of the "Semyonovskoe" Regiment (centre-left), musketeer of the "Izmailovsky" Regiment (centre-right) and grenadier of the "Preobrazhenskoe" Regiment (right) wearing the uniform used during 1786-1796.

The uniforms worn by the jager companies of the Imperial Guard's infantry during 1770-1786, from left to right: "Preobrazhenskoe" Regiment, "Semyonovskoe" Regiment and "Izmailovsky" Regiment.

(Top left) Uniforms of the Imperial Guard's cavalry during the late reign of Empress Catherine, from left to right: trooper of the "Life-Guards" Horse Regiment, trooper of the "Cavalier-Guards" in ceremonial dress and trooper of the "Life-Hussars" Squadron. The uniform of the "Life-Guards" Horse Regiment was modified in 1788.

(Top right) Trooper of the "Cavalier-Guards" wearing the ornate ceremonial uniform used during 1764-1796. Note the profusion of coloured feathers on the metal helmet and the rich decorative embroiderings.

(Left) Troopers of the "Life-Guards" Horse Regiment wearing the new uniform introduced in 1788.

(Top left) Trooper (left) and trumpeter (right) of the "Life-Hussars" Squadron, wearing the uniform used during 1775-1796.

(Top right) Trooper of the "Life-Cossacks" Squadron, wearing the uniform used during 1775-1790.

(Right) Trooper (left) and officer (right) of the "Life-Cossacks" Squadron, wearing the uniform used during 1790-1796.

(Above left) Grenadier (left) and musketeer (right) of the Gatchina Troops. The latter wore peculiar uniforms, designed by the future Tsar Paul I; when he became Emperor in 1796, the uniforms of the Gatchina Troops – with some slight modifications – were adopted by the whole Russian Army. The dark green double-breasted coat shown here, for example, became standard issue for the Russian line infantry during the Napoleonic War. The frontal plate of the grenadier's "mitre" cap shows the badge of the Russian naval infantry since the grenadier unit of the Gatchina Troops was originally recruited from marines.

(Above right) Jager of the Gatchina Troops, wearing the uniform that was later adopted by the "Life-Guards Jager Battalion".

(Left) Cuirassier of the Gatchina Troops.

(Right) Dragoon of the Gatchina Troops.

re-trained according to Prussian practices under his personal supervision.

The private army maintained by the young Paul became known as "Gatchina Troops", since it was stationed on the future Tsar's large estate of Gatchina. Paul clothed and drilled his "personal" soldiers by following the regulations promulgated by Frederick the Great almost 25 years before; according to his plans, the Gatchina Troops would have acted as an example to follow for the rest of the Russian Army. In reality, however, what Paul produced was a very outdated military corps which members were forced to return to automaton-like drill and old-fashioned uniforms that would have been perfect for the period of the Seven Years' War. The "return to the past" sponsored by the future Tsar had some negative consequences for the Russian Army, especially after Paul succeeded to his mother and ordered to re-train the whole Russian military forces like the Gatchina Troops. Paul's measures were exaggerated in most cases, since they transformed training into a sort of torture: in order to make his soldiers look like Prussian veterans, he ordered to fit steel plates around their knees and made them march stiff-legged. He also ordered the filling with shot of the hollowed musket-butts in order to produce a rattle whilst drilling.

Luckily for the Russian Army the reign of Paul I was extremely short and thus his planned reforms were never completed. The Gatchina Troops were created in 1786, initially by recruiting soldiers who belonged to the naval infantry and later by employing soldiers who had retired from active service in the army. By 1796 they had been greatly expanded and comprised the following units: five battalions of musketeers, one battalion of grenadiers, one company of Jägers, one regiment of cuirassiers, one regiment of carabiniers (heavy cavalry), one regiment of dragoons, one regiment of hussars, one regiment of Don Cossacks, three companies of foot artillery and one company of horse artillery.

The first battalion of musketeers was formed by assembling together the first three infantry companies of the Gatchina Troops in 1788; in 1796, when the latter was disbanded, its members were absorbed into the "Preobrazhensky" Regiment. The second battalion of musketeers was created in 1792 and its members were absorbed into the "Semyonovsky" Regiment in 1796; the third battalion of musketeers was raised in 1793 and its members were absorbed into the "Preobrazhensky" Regiment in 1796. The fourth battalion and the fifth battalion were formed only in 1796 and thus were quite short-lived; the first was absorbed into the "Preobrazhensky" Regiment, while the second was absorbed into the "Izmailovsky" Regiment. The single grenadier battalion was organized in 1792 and its members became part of the "Izmailovsky" Regiment in 1796. The Jäger company was raised in 1793 and contributed to the formation of the new "Life Guards Jager Battalion" in 1796. The three heavy cavalry units of the Gatchina Troops, despite being titled as "regiments", had small internal establishments: the cuirassiers, formed in 1787, consisted of a single squadron; the carabiniers, formed in 1792, consisted of a single squadron; the dragoons, formed in 1792, consisted of two squadrons.

Following the disbandment of the Gatchina Troops, all the latter's heavy cavalrymen were absorbed into the "Life Guards" Horse Regiment of the Imperial Guard. The hussars, raised in 1792 and consisting of two squadrons, became the second squadron of the Imperial Guard's "Life-Hussars" in 1796; the Cossacks, raised in 1793 and consisting of a single squadron, became the second squadron of the Imperial Guard's "Life Cossacks" in 1796. The four companies of artillery, organized during 1786-1787, became part of the new "Life Guards Artillery Battalion" that was created in 1796. As clear from the above, Paul I had a high opinion of his Gatchina Troops and thus decided to include them into the elite Imperial Guard after he succeeded his mother.

<u>Line Infantry and Jägers</u>

According to the general organization confirmed on 14 February 1763, the line infantry of the Russian Army was to consist of 4 grenadier regiments and 46 musketeer regiments. Each grenadier regiment mustered

The Russian Army of 1696 - 1796

(Left) Hussar of the Gatchina Troops.

(Right) Don Cossack of the Gatchina Troops.

(Left) Foot artilleryman of the Gatchina Troops, wearing the uniform that was later adopted by the "Life-Guards Artillery Battalion".

(Right) Horse artilleryman of the Gatchina Troops.

(Left) Musketeer officer of the line infantry, wearing the uniform used during 1763-1786. This, differently from the previous one, had red frontal lapels. On campaign, especially during hot months, it was common practice to wear only the red waistcoat that had dark green folded collar and round cuffs.

(Right) Grenadier private (left) and NCO (right) of the line infantry, wearing the uniform used during 1763-1786. The new model of "mitre" cap showed a strong Prussian influence.

(Left) Musicians of the line infantry, wearing the uniform used during 1763-1786. The dress of musicians had additional white braiding and piping; quite often it was in reversed colours, i.e. red with dark green facings.

(Right) Gunner of the artillery sections attached to the line infantry regiments, wearing the uniform used during 1763-1786. The facings and frontal lapels are black like for all the artillery units.

two battalions with six grenadier companies each, while each musketeer regiment mustered two battalions with one grenadier company and five musketeer companies each. All the line infantry regiments had the usual artillery section, which remained a peculiarity of the Russian foot troops since most of the other European armies had already disbanded the artillery detachments included into their line infantry.

During September-October 1769, by following a military fashion that was quite strong in the contemporary European armies, the Russian authorities decided to raise two multi-tasking "legions" inside their military forces. These were to comprise sub-units of infantry, cavalry and artillery in order to act as self-sufficient "miniature armies"; one legion would have been formed for Saint Petersburg and one would have been formed for Moscow, but there were plans to re-organize the whole Russian Army on "mixed" legions. Both the "Saint Petersburg's Legion" and the "Moscow's Legion" had the following internal establishment: one battalion of grenadiers, three battalions of musketeers, one company of Jägers, four squadrons of carabiniers (heavy cavalry), two squadrons of hussars, one squadron of Cossacks, one company of artillery and a detachment of engineer officers. The "experiment" represented by the two legions did not last for long, since they were disbanded on 16 January 1775 and their men were used to raise four new line infantry regiments. Meanwhile, since November 1769, a small detachment of Jägers had been added to each line infantry regiment.

The "Ukrainian Land Militia", which despite its official denomination was made up of Russians, was reorganized by Catherine the Great on 15 December 1763. It came to comprise ten infantry regiments and one cavalry regiment; the first had two battalions each like standard musketeer regiments, while the second had five squadrons with two companies each. In 1769 a second regiment of cavalry (dragoons) was formed inside the Ukrainian Land Militia. On 8 November 1770, due to the fact that Ukraine was going to be formally annexed by Russia and thus there was no longer a frontier to defend in southern Russia, the foot component of the Ukrainian Land Militia was disbanded. Its ten regiments were absorbed into the regular line infantry of the Russian Army.

By 1775 also the cavalry component of the Ukrainian Land Militia was no longer in existence, having been converted into a regular regiment of dragoons. The three dragoon regiments (mounted infantry) that made up the "Trans-Kama Land Militia" were abolished in 1771; their members were used to form 25 new units known as "Light Field Detachments". The latter were "mini-legions" comprising infantry, cavalry and artillery that were designed to operate in an autonomous way on the Russian steppe frontier (being deployed in Astrakhan, Orenburg and Siberia). Each "Light Field Detachment" was to consist of two musketeer companies, one company of Jägers, one company of dragoons (mounted infantry) and one company/battery of light artillery. Already on 22 February 1775, however, the Light Field Detachments were all disbanded: their musketeer companies were used to form eight independent line infantry battalions with four companies each (known as "Field Battalions" and tasked with guarding the Asian frontiers of Russia), while their Jäger companies were used to form two battalions of "Siberian Jägers" having four companies each. As we have already seen, since 1769 each Russian line infantry

Uniforms of the Russian foot troops from the early reign of Catherine the Great, from left to right: musketeers of the line infantry, Jagers of the light infantry, infantry officer of the Ukraine Land Militia, grenadier of the Ukraine Land Militia and artillery officer of the Ukraine Land Militia.

Grenadier of the "Ukraine Land Militia", wearing the uniform used during 1763-1770. This was white with pink facings for the foot units.

Gunner of the "Ukraine Land Militia", wearing the uniform used during 1763-1770. This was white with black facings for the artillery sections. Before 1763 the "Ukraine Land Militia" was dressed very similarly to the line infantry, in dark green.

Musketeer drummer (left) and musketeer (right) of Saint Petersburg's Legion. The two crossed anchors reproduced on the front of the headgear are the symbol of Saint Petersburg.

Grenadier (left) and jager (right) of Saint Petersburg's Legion. The "mitre" cap of the grenadier has the frontal plate covered with fur, in order to look like a bearskin.

Carabinier of Saint Petersburg's Legion

Hussar trooper (left) and NCO (right) of Saint Petersburg's Legion. For service dress, the black "mirliton" shako was often replaced with a black bicorn (especially by officers and NCOs).

(Top Left) Carabinier NCO (left) and officer (right) of Moscow's Legion.

(Top Right) Hussar officer (left) and trooper (right) of Moscow's Legion.

(Bottom Left) Cossack NCO (left), trooper (centre) and officer (right) of Moscow's Legion.

(Bottom Right) Artilleryman of Moscow's Legion.

regiment comprised one detachment of light infantrymen armed with rifled carbines. Jägers had been introduced into the Russian Army after conducting a series of experiments on the border with Finland, where the local terrain was not well suited to the employment of line infantry or cavalry.

A first "experimental corps" of Jägers, made up of Finnish hunters, was created during 1763-1764; the new unit – numbering 300 men - soon showed to the Russian military commanders how a light infantry corps could move very rapidly on broken terrain and how it could fight in the woods for conducting scouting or skirmishing operations. A special commission was formed by Catherine the Great to evaluate the performances of the new light infantrymen; following the success of the experimental corps, it was decided to form a small detachment of Jägers in each line infantry unit (5 men were chosen from each company of grenadiers and musketeers to create such detachments). The youngest and fittest line infantrymen were selected to be re-trained as light infantrymen; most of these were already the best marksmen of their respective companies. On 26 May 1777 the various Jäger detachments existing in the Russian line infantry were separated from their parent units and assembled together in order to form six independent "Jäger Corps" mustering four battalions with four companies each.

During 1777-1784 several new "Field Battalions" were created inside the Russian infantry, especially for garrisoning the newly acquired Ukrainian territories; 1786, instead, saw the formation of a new Jager Corps. By 1786 the Russian foot troops had been significantly enlarged by Catherine the Great and thus consisted of the following units: 10 regiments of grenadiers, 55 regiments of line infantry, 15 Field Battalions, 7 Jäger Corps and 2 battalions of Siberian Jägers. In 1786 a general reorganization of the Russian infantry's internal structure was carried on; according to it, each grenadier regiment was to consist of four battalions with four grenadier companies; each musketeer regiment, instead, was to consist of two battalions with one grenadier company and five musketeer companies each. Just a few line infantry regiments, serving in border areas, had a different internal establishment with four battalions of four musketeer companies each. Each Field Battalion was to have six companies, while a single Jäger Corps was to consist of four battalions with six companies each. The two battalions of Siberian Jägers had six companies each. The final years of Catherine the Great's long reign saw a further expansion of the Russian foot troops and some minor organizational changes. By 1796 the Russian infantry consisted of the following corps: 12 regiments of grenadiers, 55 regiments of line infantry, 20 Field Battalions, 10 Jäger Corps and 3 independent battalions of Jägers. Each of the grenadier regiments now had five battalions with five companies, while the internal composition of the other kinds of foot units was not altered.

Officer (left) and NCO (right) of the jagers, wearing the uniform used during 1764-1777. The dress shown here was modified only slightly when the jagers were detached from their parent units and thus, in practice, it continued to be used until 1786.

Musician of the jagers, wearing the uniform used during 1764-1777.

(Top Left) Cossack officer of Saint Petersburg's Legion. (Top Right) Artilleryman (left), artillery officers (centre) and engineer officer (right) of Saint Petersburg's Legion. (Bottom left) Jager (left) and musketeer (right) of Moscow's Legion. The headgear of the musketeer bears the initials of Moscow on the front. (Bottom Right) Grenadiers of Moscow's Legion. In this case, the headgear is a true bearskin

The Russian Army of 1696 - 1796

(Top left) Cuirassier NCO, wearing the uniform used during 1756-1762. The white dress and black cuirass showed a clear German influence.

(Top right) Cuirassier, wearing the uniform used during 1756-1762. The massive horse is of the Holstein breed.

(Bottom right) Dragoons, wearing the uniform used during 1764-1775. This was dark blue for all the regiments, including the "garrison" ones. The figure on the right is wearing the new dark green dress that was introduced in 1775.

The Heavy and Medium Cavalry

Officers (left), trumpeter (centre) and trooper (right) of the cuirassiers, wearing the uniform used during 1778-1786. In the years 1763-1778 the Russian cuirassiers wore a slightly modified version of the "German" uniform that they already used during Empress Elizabeth's reign.

On 14 January 1763 Catherine the Great decided to disband the six regiments of horse grenadiers existing inside the Russian Army and to replace them with a new category of heavy cavalrymen: the "carabiniers". The Russian Army needed to have more heavy cavalry units that could fight on equal terms against the Prussian cuirassiers and dragoons; forming new cuirassier regiments, however, would have had enormous costs that the Russian government was in no conditions to sustain. For this reason, it was decided to convert the six regiments of horse grenadiers and thirteen of the twenty existing dragoon regiments into new units of carabiniers; the latter would have been trained very similarly to the cuirassiers but unlike the latter they would have not been equipped with metal cuirasses and would have not been mounted on massive horses. The 19 new units of carabiniers formed by converting existing corps were soon increased to 20 with the formation of a new regiment. Each regiment of carabiniers consisted of five squadrons with two companies each, exactly like a standard cuirassier regiment. Following the important organizational changes described above, the Russian Army started to feel the need for more units of dragoons since most of the latter had been converted into regiments of carabiniers; as a result, on 1 May 1764, all the regiments of "garrison dragoons" were transformed into units of regular dragoons.

In 1784 a general reorganization of the Russian heavy and medium cavalry took place, after two decades that had seen several organizational changes. By that year the Russian Army comprised 5 regiments of cuirassiers, 19 regiments of carabiniers and 10 regiments of dragoons. As clear from the above, the creation and progressive enlargement of the carabiniers had caused a slight reduction of the cuirassiers and a significant one of the dragoons. According to the reorganization of 1784 each regiment of cuirassiers and each regiment of carabiniers was to have six squadrons, while each regiment of dragoons was to have ten squadrons. A single cavalry squadron continued to consist of two companies. It is important to notice that the heavy cavalry carabiniers had little in common with the light cavalry units bearing their same denomination and having been formed in Ukraine from former Zaporizhian Cossacks.

The Ukrainian light cavalry units, in order to be more distinguishable from the heavy regiments of carabiniers, soon became known as "Light Horse Regiments". On 16 October 1788 one of the existing regiments of carabiniers, which was operating in Finland against the Swedes, was converted into a

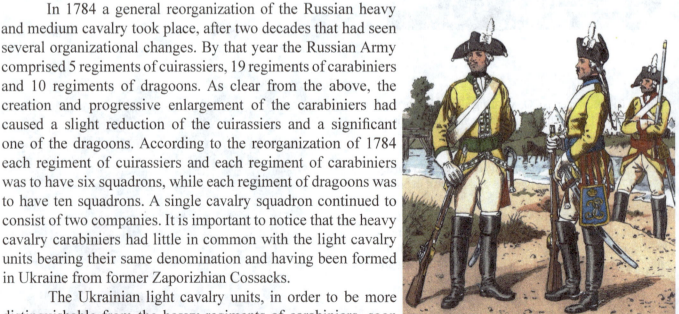

Cuirassiers wearing the uniform used during 1778-1786. The Prussian-style "koller" tunic had some distinctive bands of lace on the front and on the turnbacks.

dragoon unit; the latter had an extra-large establishment, since attached to it there were five newly raised hussar squadrons. Since 16 May 1790 one of the cuirassier regiments received the official denomination of "Prince Potemkin Cuirassiers" and started to act as the mounted bodyguard of Prince Potemkin, overall commander of the Russian Army and one of Catherine the Great's favourite lovers. Always on 16 May 1790 a new heavy cavalry unit was formed, i.e. an elite regiment of horse grenadiers that was created in Ukraine by converting an existing infantry corps; this unit, which remained as the only horse grenadier corps of the Russian Army for some time, had a large establishment with ten squadrons of two companies each.

By the time of Empress Catherine's death, in 1796, the Russian heavy and medium cavalry mustered the following units: 5 regiments of cuirassiers, 16 regiments of carabiniers, 11 regiments of dragoons and 1 regiment of horse grenadiers. The units of cuirassiers and carabiniers had six squadrons each, while those of dragoons and horse grenadiers had ten squadrons each. After his ascendancy to the throne, Tsar Paul I decided to disband the regiments of carabiniers existing inside the Russian Army: nine were converted into units of cuirassiers, six were converted into units of dragoons and one was completely cancelled. On 29 November 1796 the horse grenadier regiment was converted into a cuirassier unit; as a result, the heavy and medium cavalry of the Russian Army started to comprise only corps of cuirassiers and dragoons.

Dragoons wearing the uniform used during 1764-1775. The dress shown here was modified only slightly in 1775, when its colour was changed to dark green. The new dark green uniform was used during 1775-1786.

(Top Left) Carabinier wearing the uniform used during 1763-1778.

(Top Right) Carabinier trumpeter wearing the uniform used during 1763-1778.

(Right) Carabinier wearing the new uniform with "koller" tunic that was used during 1778-1786.

Light Cavalry

By 1742 the Russian Army comprised four regiments of regular light cavalry mostly recruited from Balkan individuals: the Serbian Hussars, the Georgian Hussars, the Hungarian Hussars and the Moldavian Hussars. The decisive expansion of the Russian Army's regular light cavalry, as we have already seen, took place during the following years and especially after the outbreak of the Seven Years' War. During the 1750s a fresh wave of Orthodox Christian communities entered the borders of Russia from the Balkans, providing new manpower sufficient to raise another four regiments of hussars: the "Slobodian Hussars" in 1756, the "Macedonian Hussars" in 1759, the "Bulgarian Hussars" in 1759 and the "Yellow Hussars" in 1760. The latter unit, which took its name from the colour of its uniform, was recruited from the Serbian communities that had already settled in Russian Ukraine during the previous decade (which members were known as "New Serbians"). As a result of the above, by 1762 the Russian Army comprised eight regiments of hussars. In addition to those active units, it could also count on some garrison corps made up of Balkan military settlers and known as "settled hussars". These were mostly Serbs and lived in the settlement known as "New Serbia", which had been established during 1751 in Russian Ukraine.

Detailed contemporary picture showing a group of Russian Cossacks during the second half of the 18th century. On the right, near the officer depicted in the centre, there is a Tatar light horseman. All the irregular cavalrymen are armed with lances and are mounted on sturdy ponies of the steppes. ASKB

In exchange for some land located along the border with Tatar Crimea, the Serbian military settlers were required to form some military units. The military settlers were tasked with patrolling the frontier but were fully mobilized only in case of war. Each district of New Serbia was to supply one company of hussars as well as one company of light infantry. The hussar companies were 40 in total: 20 were active companies and 20 were reserve companies that could be mobilized in case of need. The 40 companies were assembled into two regiments, known as "1st Hussars of New Serbia" and "2nd Hussars of New Serbia".

In 1753, following the example of New Serbia, a new settlement inhabited by Balkan refugees was formed in Russian Ukraine; this was known as "Slavonic Serbia" and was inhabited by Serbians coming from Slavonia. The Russian authorities wanted to use the settlements of New Serbia and Slavonic Serbia as buffer zones between their southern territories and the Ottoman lands by following the model of the Austrian "Grenz" or "Military Border" in the Balkans. As a result, also the settlers of Slavonic Serbia were assigned some land in exchange for being required to form some military units. As it had happened with New Serbia, the entire male population was registered for military service; the Slavonian refugees were to provide one company of hussars for each of the districts that made up their settlement. Two regiments of Slavonian hussars were thus raised, each having 10 active companies and 10 reserve companies; both units were named after their commanders: "Shevich Hussars" and "Preradovich Hussars". Soon after the end of the Seven Years' War, the light infantry units recruited from the settlers of New Serbia were all disbanded and thus the Balkan communities living on the

Trooper of the Serbian Hussars, wearing the uniform used during 1742-1762.

Officer of the Georgian Hussars, wearing the uniform used during 1742-1762.

Trooper of the Slobodian Hussars, wearing the uniform used during 1742-1762.

(Top Left) Trumpeter of the Hungarian Hussars (left) and trooper of the Georgian Hussars (right), wearing the uniform that was used during 1763-1776.

(Top Right) Officer (left) and troopers (right) of the Black Hussars and Yellow Hussars, wearing the uniform that was used during 1763-1776.

(Bottom Left) Hussars of the new regiments raised in March 1765 from former Ukrainian Cossacks, wearing the uniform that was used during 1763-1776. This was modified only slightly in 1776 and thus, in practice, it continued to be used until the temporary disappearance of all the hussar units in 1783.

(Left) Hussar officer of one of the new regiments raised in March 1765 from former Ukrainian Cossacks, wearing the uniform used during 1776-1783.

(Right) Officer (left) and trooper (right) of the "Voronez" Hussar Regiment, wearing the uniform used during 1788-1796.

Russian territory continued to provide only hussars.

During 1762-1763 the eight regular regiments of hussars were partly reorganized: the Bulgarian Hussars were disbanded and absorbed into the Macedonian Hussars, while the Yellow Hussars were disbanded and absorbed into the Georgian Hussars. Very soon, however, also the Macedonian Hussars were disbanded due to their shortage of personnel. As a result, five regiments of regular hussars remained: the Serbian Hussars, the Georgian Hussars, the Hungarian Hussars, the Moldavian Hussars and the Slobodian Hussars. These all had eight squadrons each, except for the last one that mustered five squadrons with two companies each. In the early months of 1765, the Moldavian Hussars were given the new official denomination of Samara Hussars, while a new regiment of regular hussars – the Bakhmut Hussars – was created by assembling together the Shevich Hussars and Preradovich Hussars of Slavonic Serbs.

In the late months of 1764, the ten regiments that made up the "City Army" of the Cossack Hetmanate - with a few exceptions - were all disbanded and their members were assembled together with the Balkan settlers living on the territory of Ukraine in the settlements of New Serbia and Slavonic Serbia to form six new regiments of regular light cavalry. The latter consisted of two hussar regiments, known as "Black Hussars" and "Yellow Hussars", that were mostly recruited from the Balkan communities and of four lancer regiments that were mostly recruited from Zaporizhian Cossacks. Each of the new lancer units consisted of 16 mounted companies and 4 infantry companies; in time of war the former were assembled into 8 squadrons with two companies each, while the latter were to serve as garrison units.

On 3 March 1765, by recruiting more former Cossacks of the Zaporizhian Army, the Russian authorities could raise another five regiments of regular hussars. These were all named after some major Ukrainian cities and consisted of six squadrons each. Following the creation of these new units, the Samara Hussars were disbanded and absorbed into the Bakhmut Hussars. In 1769 the Georgian Hussars were disbanded, and their members were absorbed into the short-lived "Moscow's Legion". After the disbandment of both the "Saint Petersburg's Legion" and the "Moscow's Legion", the hussars who had been part of the latter units were assembled together in order to form a new regular regiment of "Belarussian Hussars".

Following the Russian annexation of the former Cossack Hetmanate, on 9 September 1775, a new hussar regiment was created by assembling together the Black Hussars with the Yellow Hussars and was given the official denomination of "Ukrainian Hussars". As a result of the above changes, by the end of 1775 the Russian Army comprised the following units of hussars: Serbian Hussars, Hungarian Hussars, Slobodian Hussars, Bakhmut Hussars, Belarusian Hussars, Ukrainian Hussars and the five regiments organized in March 1765 from former Cossacks.

On 24 December 1776 the eleven hussar units listed above were reorganized as eight "consolidated" regiments: the Serbian Hussars, the Hungarian Hussars, the Moldavian Hussars, the Wallachian Hussars, the Bulgarian Hussars, the Macedonian Hussars, the Illyrian Hussars and the Dalmatian Hussars. It is interesting to note how several of the new units bore the name of hussar regiments that had been disbanded just a few years before.

The years 1775-1776 saw some major organizational changes inside the Russian light cavalry, which started to comprise some new units in addition to those of hussars described above. Following the disappearance of the Cossack Hetmanate, in fact, the three "mercenary" regiments of Ukrainian Cossacks that had been in Russian service since the years of the Great Northern War were reorganized as three regular light cavalry regiments. Each of the latter had six squadrons and was named after the city in which it was garrisoned: 1st "Kiev" Light Horse Regiment, 2nd "Siversk" Light Horse Regiment and 3rd "Chernihiv" Light Horse Regiment. In addition to the above, during 1776 also the last surviving regiment of the Zaporizhian "City Army" was disbanded by the Russians and thus the latter could raise some more units of regular lancers from former Zaporizhian Cossacks. Two new regiments were added to the existing ones, bringing the total of Ukrainian lancer units included into the Russian Army to six. According to the new internal organization introduced in 1776, each regiment of lancers was to consist of six squadrons with two mounted companies each.

Ukrainian NCO (left) and officer (right) from one of the lancer regiments raised by the Russians from former Zaporizhian Cossacks in 1764. The uniform shown here was worn until 1776.

Ukrainian trooper from one of the lancer regiments raised by the Russians from former Zaporizhian Cossacks in 1764. The headgear made of fur and the use of the lance show a certain Cossack influence, while the white colour of the coat is reminiscent of the Ukraine Land Militia's dress.

(Left) Ukrainian trooper from one of the lancer regiments raised by the Russians from former Zaporizhian Cossacks in 1764. The three Ukrainian Light Horse regiments formed by the Russians from the former Zaporizhian "Lowland Army" were dressed quite similarly to this figure, but with red coat having facings in regimental colour (yellow for the 1st "Kiev" Light Horse Regiment, blue for the 2nd "Siversk" Light Horse Regiment and green for the 3rd "Chernihiv" Light Horse Regiment).

(Right) Ukrainian trumpeter from one of the lancer regiments raised by the Russians from former Zaporizhian Cossacks in 1764. The "Companion Banner" acting as the mounted bodyguard of the Zaporizhian Hetman was given a regular "hussar-style" uniform in 1752 that consisted of black "mirliton" shako, red "dolman" jacket, medium blue "pelisse" trimmed with black fur and red trousers.

In 1783, following the annexation of the Crimean Khanate to Ukraine, the Russians decided to reorganize their regular Ukrainian cavalry units. The three regiments of "Light Horse" that had been "regularized" in 1775 were retained in service but received the new official denomination of "Carabiniers"; the six regiments of lancers, instead, were assembled together in couples to form three new regiments of regular Cossacks. Always in 1783 another six new regiments of Cossacks were created, by assembling together the existing corps of regular hussars: one regiment from the Hungarian Hussars and Moldavian Hussars, one regiment from the Serbian Hussars and Bulgarian Hussars, one regiment from the Illyrian Hussars and Wallachian Hussars, one regiment from the Macedonian Hussars and Dalmatian Hussars and one regiment from a temporary hussar corps made up of former Zaporizhian Cossacks. Each of the new regiments had six squadrons with two companies each. Just a few months after their formation, the new units received the new official denomination of "Carabiniers" and thus became "Light Horse" regiments.

Following the above changes, the Russian Army no longer comprised any unit of hussars or lancers; its light cavalry component, in fact, started to consist of 12 Light Horse regiments (the three ones that had been "regularized" in 1775, the three that had been formed from lancer corps in 1775 and the six that had been formed from hussar corps in 1783). The number of Light Horse regiments was soon increased to 13 with the formation of a new unit. On 10 April 1786 the standard internal establishment of all the Light Horse regiments was fixed at six squadrons; since 25 January 1788 a small detachment of Horse Jägers was added to each of the existing Light Horse regiments.

Ukrainian trooper from one of the lancer regiments raised by the Russians from former Zaporizhian Cossacks since 1764. He is wearing the new Cossack-style uniform that was introduced in 1776 and continued to be used until 1784. The new "Life-Company" created during 1764 in the Zaporizhian Host to replace the "Companion Banner" was dressed with a conventional uniform, almost identical to that of the contemporary Russian line infantry: black tricorn, dark blue coat with red frontal lapels and facings, red waistcoat and breeches.

Ukrainian trumpeter (left) and trooper (right) from one of the lancer regiments raised by the Russians from former Zaporizhian Cossacks since 1764. They are both wearing the new uniform used during 1776-1784. The latter was based on the traditional dress of the Zaporizhian Cossacks, whose "City Army" never adopted regular uniforms but always wore civilian clothes.

Officer of the Don Cossacks.

Kalmyk light horseman, armed with a Mongolic composite bow.

Trooper of the Don Cossacks. The various Cossack units started to receive "regular" uniforms only during the Napoleonic Wars.

In August 1788, following the outbreak of war with Sweden, the Russian authorities decided to raise a new regiment of hussars in Saint Petersburg; the latter, however, was never formed due to the shortage of manpower and thus only five independent squadrons of hussars could be organized. These were soon attached to the "Pskov" Dragoon Regiment that was operating against the Swedes in Finland and thus never became an independent corps. After having been without hussars for some years, the Russian Army started to feel an increasing need for new hussar corps; as a result, in the last months of 1788, two of the existing Light Horse regiments – the "Voronez" and the "Olviopol" – were converted into hussar units. At the same time, in Moscow, two independent squadrons of hussars were raised in order to act as the mounted urban police of the Russian capital.

The last years of Catherine the Great's reign saw a progressive expansion of the Horse Jägers, which were detached from their parent units of Light Horse in order to form four independent regiments (raised during 1789-1790). The Horse Jägers were armed with rifled carbines and were trained to act like their infantry equivalents; being mounted infantrymen, however, they had a higher degree of mobility. Each of the four regiments of Horse Jägers was structured on ten squadrons having two companies each. By 1796 the regular light cavalry of the Russian Army consisted of the following corps: 2 regiments of hussars, 7 independent squadrons of hussars, 11 regiments of Light Horse and 4 regiments of Horse Jägers.

Cossacks

During Catherine the Great's long reign the organization of the Cossack cavalry and of the other "irregular" mounted troops of the Russian Army did not change in a significant way, except for the formation of some temporary corps that were created by recruiting Balkan refugees who had entered the Russian territory after having fought against the Ottomans. On 12 February 1785, by recruiting Moldavian and Wallachian refugees who had sided with Russia during the last Russo-Ottoman War, a new Cossack regiment was formed; this was known as "Bug Cossacks", since its members settled along the course of the Bug River. In 1786 the corps was split into two regiments. Always in 1786, in order to accelerate their penetration into the Caucasus, the Russians decided to organize five communities of "settled Cossacks" in Georgia; these were tasked with guarding the Caucasian frontier of the Russian Empire and included the Volga Cossacks, who had ceased to be a Host and had moved to the Caucasus. In 1787 a new Host was created in Ukraine, in order to replace the former Zaporizhian one; this assumed the denomination of Yekaterinoslav Host and soon absorbed the regiments of Bug Cossacks.

Always in 1787 two short-lived "brigades" of Cossacks were raised from new Balkan refugees and the new "Black Sea Cossack Host" was created from former Zaporizhian Cossacks. The Black Sea Cossacks were transferred to the Caucasus in 1792, where they settled along the course of the Kuban River. In 1793 the Chuguev Cossacks were reorganized on three regiments, the first of which acted as the guard of Prince Potemkin's personal convoy. The three units of Chuguev Cossacks were among the few ones to be placed on the regular establishment of the Russian Army. By 1796 several of the minor Cossack Hosts existing during the previous decades had been disbanded and thus only the following six remained: the Don Host, the Yekaterinoslav Host, the Black Sea Host, the Orenburg Host, the Astrakhan Host and the Siberian Host. The last three had originally been created as smaller Cossack communities and became Hosts only after the Russians expanded their possessions in Siberia. The Orenburg Host provided four regular regiments to the Russian Army (one of which was mostly made up of Bashkirs), while the Astrakhan Host provided a single regular regiment. In the Caucasus there was a single regiment of regular Cossacks, provided by the Terek Cossacks.

Bashkir heavy horseman, equipped with metal helmet and cuirass of chainmail. ASKB

Artillery and Technical Corps

Catherine the Great reorganized the Russian artillery on 3 April 1763, adopting a general structure that remained almost unchanged until the end of her reign. According to it, the Russian artillery was to consist of five major units: 1st Gunner Regiment, 2nd Gunner Regiment, Bombardier Regiment, 1st Fusilier Regiment and 2nd Fusilier Regiment. Each of the latter was to consist of five companies, which corresponded to batteries for the Gunner Regiments and for the Bombardier Regiment. As previously, the two Gunner Regiments were equipped with field guns while the Bombardier Regiment operated howitzers; the Fusilier Regiments were tasked with protecting the artillery batteries on the battlefield and thus were "special" infantry units. In 1793 the Russian artillery was enlarged with the formation of three independent Bombardier Battalions, which were equipped with howitzers and were tasked with conducting besieging operations.

In 1794 the first horse artillery corps of the Russian Army were created, consisting of five independent companies equipped with light horse-drawn field guns. Generally speaking, the "traditional" foot artillery moved very slowly on the battlefields and changed position very rarely during a clash. To go beyond these tactical limits, during the Seven Years' War the Prussian monarch Frederick the Great decided to develop a new form of artillery that would have been capable of moving much more rapidly on the battlefields thanks to the use of lighter guns drawn by horses. Initially Frederick's idea seemed to be a complete failure, since it was too innovative for the contemporary standards; with the progression of time, however, it became clear that the new horse-drawn artillery could have an enormous tactical potential. As opposed to the foot artillery, horse batteries could be deployed very easily to the points of the battlefield where their presence was needed; in addition, they could also support the attacks launched by the cavalry since they could move at the same pace of the horsemen. Obviously creating a new branch of service from zero was not something simple: new and lighter guns, specifically designed for the horse batteries, had to be created; in addition, both the artillerymen and the horses of the new mounted batteries had to undergo some specific training. New horse-drawn carriages were developed and some specific tactics for the employment of mounted artillery were formulated. By the outbreak of the French Revolutionary Wars, horse artillery was already a "stable presence" in most of the major European armies. Prussia, for example, had three companies of horse artillery by 1792.

Several other nations - like Russia - followed Frederick the Great's example during the last decades of the 18th century and thus organized their own units of mounted artillery. Until the end of Empress Catherine's reign each line infantry regiment of the Russian Army continued to comprise one section of artillery; with the progression of time, however, the latter lost most of its original tactical significance. In addition to the units described above, the Russian artillery did comprise also several "garrison" companies and detachments that were scattered across the vast territory of the Russian Empire.

For what regards the minor technical corps, the single Pontoon Company continued to exist after the reorganization of 1763, being attached to the artillery. In 1790 a second company of pontoniers was created to supplement the

Gunner (left) and drummer (right) of the field artillery, wearing the uniform used during 1763-1786. This, differently from the previous one, had black frontal lapels.

(Left) Gunner of the field artillery, wearing the new "Potemkin uniform" used during 1786-1796.

(Right) Bombardier wearing the uniform used during 1763-1786. Note the peculiar grenadier-style cap. In 1786 also the bombardiers adopted the new "Potemkin uniform".

(Bottom left) Officer of the Horse Artillery, wearing the uniform used during 1794-1796.

(Bottom right) Trooper of the Horse Artillery, wearing the uniform used during 1794-1796.

(Top left) Engineer officer (left), pioneer (centre) and miner (right) of the Engineer Corps, wearing the uniform used during 1763 - 1786

(Top right) Private (left) and officer (right) of the Miner Company from the Engineer Corps, wearing the new "Potemkin uniform" used during 1786-1796.

(Left) Privates (left) and NCO (right) of the Pontinier Corps, wearing the uniform used during 1771-1775. Before 1771 and after 1775 the pontoniers were dressed like the gunners of the field artillery.

existing ones. In 1763 the Engineer Corps was reorganized on one company of miners and one company of sappers, which served as the "labour force" of the engineer officers. On 17 October 1793 an independent "Engineer Company for the Southern Borders" was raised for service in the Caucasus area.

Garrison troops

For what regards garrison troops Empress Catherine, as we have already seen, transformed the "garrison dragoons" into regular dragoons; in addition, on 19 April 1764, she ordered to re-structure all the "garrison infantry" units as 84 independent battalions. The latter were divided into two main categories: "Border Garrison Battalions" (serving on the frontiers) and "Internal Garrison Battalions" (serving in the interior provinces). Each of the first had four active companies, one company of auxiliary workers and one company of invalids/veterans; each of the second had five active companies and one company of invalids/veterans. By 1796 the garrison battalions of the Russian Army had been increased to 106, including five that were stationed in Saint Petersburg and three that were stationed in Moscow. The garrison troops of the Russian Army, in addition to the infantry battalions described above, did comprise also some units that were specifically tasked with guarding the most important mines of their country. These were organized by Catherine the Great since 1762 and by 1796 consisted of two battalions plus four independent companies of infantry.

Private (left) and NCO (right) of the Garrison Battalions, wearing the uniform used during 1764-1786. In 1786 the dress shown here was replaced with the new "Potemkin uniform".

Some important institutions of the Russian state, including some private ones, had their own "autonomous" guard detachments that were all part – at least formally – of the Russian Army. The Governing Senate, the most important executive body of the Russian Empire that was established by Peter the Great, had its own guard consisting of two infantry companies since December 1763. In 1764 the latter were expanded and reorganized as a new unit that became known as "Battalion of the Senate". In May 1764 a small infantry detachment was assigned to the "Educational Society for Noble-Born Girls" that existed in Saint Petersburg; in September of the same year a single infantry company was created to guard the War Commissariat of the Russian Army. In 1765 the so-called "Office for the Construction of Buildings and Gardens", which was responsible for the construction and maintenance of the imperial buildings, was assigned two infantry battalions having five companies each

Musketeer (left) and dragoon (right) of the "Mines' Troops", wearing the uniform used during 1764-1786. In 1786 the dress shown here was replaced with the new "Potemkin uniform"

Musketeer of the "Battalion of the Senate". | Officer of the infantry company guarding the War Commissariat. | Musketeer of the infantry company guarding the Provision Commissariat.

(Left) Musketeer (left) and grenadier (right) of the infantry battalions assigned to the "Office for the Construction of Buildings and Gardens"

(Right) Officer (left) and musketeer (right) of the infantry detachment assigned to the Ministry of Foreign Affairs. Both the infantry detachment of the "Noble Bank" of Saint Petersburg and the infantry company of the "Trinity Company" were dressed like the regular line infantry but in dark blue with yellow facings.

(one of grenadiers, three of musketeers and one of auxiliary workers). In 1766 a single infantry company was created to guard the Provision Commissariat of the Russian Army. In 1772 a small infantry detachment was assigned to the "Salt Office" of Saint Petersburg, which was responsible for the administration of all the Russian salt mines. In 1773 a single infantry company was created for the maintenance of the Kremlin in Moscow; in 1774 the "Noble Bank" of Saint Petersburg, where most of the Russian aristocrats had their fortunes, was assigned a small infantry detachment. In 1775 the "Trinity Company", i.e. the newly-created Russian commercial company that was tasked with trading with the Chinese Empire, was assigned an infantry company and a small detachment of Cossacks. Always in 1775 the Court Chancellery was assigned an infantry detachment; the same was done for the Ministry of Foreign Affairs in 1779. In 1785 a small foot guard was assigned to the "Patrimonial Estates Department", which was tasked with the administration of the imperial family's land properties. In 1795 an infantry detachment was created for guarding the "Imperial Foundry of Donetsk", one of the most important foundries of the Russian Empire.

Greek Troops

Catherine the Great fought two major wars against the Ottoman Empire: the first in 1768-1774 and the second in 1787-1792. These were particularly important, because they led to the Russian annexation of the Crimean Khanate as well as to the beginning of a more effective Russian penetration into the Caucasus. During the two Russo-Turkish Wars of the late 18th century the Christian peoples of the Balkans, which lived under Ottoman control since centuries, sided with the Russians hoping to receive the latter's support in their struggles from freedom. The Greeks, in particular, established solid diplomatic relations with the Russian Empire with the objective of forming a strong anti-Turkish military alliance. Empress Catherine, after conquering Crimea, was greatly interested in obtaining an outlet to the Mediterranean Sea for her country and thus saw the formation of an alliance with the Greeks as an opportunity to send the Russian Navy to the Mediterranean. The Russian Empire started to present itself as the defender of all the Orthodox Christians living in the Balkans, using religious contrasts as a "casus belli" to attack the Turks in their own territories.

NCO (left) and privates (right) from the 1st Battalion of the Greek Infantry Regiment, wearing the uniform used during 1779-1796.

Under Ottoman rule the Greeks had developed some irregular military forces, which mostly consisted of mountaineers equipped like light infantrymen; these were divided into two main categories: "klephtes" and "armatoloi". The first resisted Turkish rule by operating as brigands in the countryside areas, while the second acted as "rural policemen" on behalf of the Ottomans in order to contrast the activities of the "klephtes". Following the outbreak of hostilities between the Russian Empire and the Ottoman Empire in 1768, the Russian government sent some agents to Greece in order to favour the outbreak of local anti-Turkish revolts by spreading pro-Russia propaganda. The activities of the Russian agents had great success, since they led to the formation of alliances between the Russian Empire and some important "brotherhoods" of Greek "klephtes" like those of the Maniates and of the Souliotes.

In 1770, while the Turks were fighting against the Russians in Crimea, a major Greek uprising broke out in the Peloponnese region; this was ignited by the arrival of a Russian fleet, which conducted a series of landings on the Greek coastline. Very soon the Russians started to form some auxiliary military units from the Greek insurgents who joined them; an "Eastern Spartan Legion" and a "Western Spartan Legion", having around 1,000 men each, were soon organized from Maniates. This first Greek "national" uprising, however, was soon crushed by the Turks after the Russian warships had to abandon the Mediterranean Sea in order to operate on other fronts. In any case, several of the insurgents who had fought alongside the Russians found refuge and employment as sailors on the vessels of the Russian Navy. These refugees initially numbered 3,000 and included significant numbers of Montenegrins and Dalmatians in addition to Greeks.

In December 1771 the Russian authorities decided to assemble the best elements of these former insurgents – 1,500 men – into five light infantry battalions known as "Albanian Battalions". Each of the latter mustered 300 men and was made up of individuals coming from a different region: the first was made up of individuals coming from the island of Cephalonia, the second was made up of individuals coming from the island of Zante, the third was made up of Albanians, the fourth was made up of individuals coming from the Greek region of Morea and the fifth was made up of Maniates. Despite their lack of discipline, the members of the "Albanian Battalions" performed very well as auxiliaries of the Russian naval forces by conducting effective landings and raids. By 1774 the number of "Albanian Battalions" had been increased to 11 and each of them mustered five companies.

During the years 1775-1787 the alliance existing between the Russian Empire and the Greeks became increasingly stronger: many Greek political exiles went to Russia, where they entered the ranks of the military forces and of the civil administration. The most intelligent and well-educated members of this "exiled community" became part of the Russian court, starting to influence the decisions of the Russian government in favour of Greek independence. Several Greek merchants established themselves in Ukraine, where they came to control the local trading activities; some Greek intellectuals, instead, became part of the Russian government like Ioannis Kapodistrias who was Foreign Minister of Russia during 1816-1822 before becoming the founder of the modern Greek nation.

NCO (left), private (centre) and officer (right) from the 2nd Battalion of the Greek Infantry Regiment, wearing the uniform used during 1779-1796.

During the Russo-Turkish War of 1787-1792 the Russian Navy could not send a naval squadron to the Mediterranean since it was fighting against the Swedes in the Baltic Sea; as a result, no major popular uprising took place in Greece against the Ottomans. In any case, the Greeks organized several "flotillas" that operated against the Turks and intensified their activities of "guerrilla" on land. Meanwhile, since 1775, hundreds of Greeks who were part of the "Albanian Battalions" were invited to settle in Crimea by the Russian authorities. They wanted to populate the Crimean Peninsula with some trusted and warlike communities of Orthodox Christians, since that portion of Ukraine was still mostly inhabited by Muslim Tatars who were always ready to revolt against the new Russian regime. The Greek soldiers who decided to settle in Crimea together with their families enjoyed a series of privileges: they received funds for the construction of their new houses, they were exempted from the payment of taxes, they were permitted to appoint their own religious authorities and – most importantly – they were assigned some land properties.

In 1779 the former members of the "Albanian Battalions", which had been disbanded in 1775, were re-organized as a corps of military settlers known as "Greek Infantry Regiment". This originally had 12 companies, which were soon reduced to 8 (assembled into two battalions); each company was named after a famous region of Greece. The town of Balaklava became the major urban centre of the new Greek settlements in Crimea and thus the new military unit soon started to be known as the "Balaklava Infantry Regiment". Peacetime duties of the latter included the maintaining of a coastal cordon guard for customs and quarantine duties as well as for the prevention of smuggling. During the Russo-Turkish War of 1787-1792 most of the regiment's companies served as naval infantry on the warships of the Russian Navy operating in the Black Sea. Following ascension of Tsar Paul I to the throne in 1796, the Greek military unit was reduced in its numbers and started to be known as "Balaklava Infantry Battalion"; the latter remained part of the Russian Army until its final disbandment in 1859.

After the Russo-Turkish War of 1787-1792 a new Greek military colony was established by the Russians in the Ukrainian port city of Odessa; this provided three infantry companies with 100 men each to the Russian Army, which were collectively known as "Greek Detachment of Odessa". The latter was mostly made up of former privateers who had fought at sea against the Ottomans and continued to exist until 1796, when it was disbanded by Paul I. The Greek unit was reactivated in 1803 as a battalion with four companies, the Greek corps of Odessa was dissolved in a definitive way during 1815. To conclude this overview of the Greek military presence in the Russian Army during Catherine the Great's reign, it is interesting to remember how the Empress even created a military academy for the children of Greek veterans who had fought for Russia during the Russo-Turkish Wars. This institution, known as "Cadet Corps of Foreign Co-religionists", was organized in 1774 and educated young Greek refugees for a future career in the Russian military forces. Before being de-activated in 1796, the military academy produced around 200 graduates.

Polish-Lithuanian troops

The military units of the Polish-Lithuanian Commonwealth did not disappear completely after the dissolution of their state; several of them, in fact, were not disbanded and were absorbed into the Russian Army as "foreign troops". Following the end of the "War in Defence of the Constitution" and the subsequent Second Partition of Poland, the following Polish-Lithuanian military units entered Russian service: the 11th Foot Regiment of the Polish Crown, the 12th Foot Regiment of the Polish Crown, the 5th Cavalry Brigade of the Polish Crown, the 6th Cavalry Brigade of the Polish Crown, the 7th Cavalry Brigade of the Polish Crown, the 8th Cavalry Brigade of the Polish Crown, the 2nd Advance Guard Regiment of the Polish Crown, the 4th Advance Guard Regiment of the Polish Crown, the 5th Advance Guard Regiment of the Polish Crown, the 2nd Regiment of Loyal Cossacks (one of the two Cossack units

NCO (left) and private (right) of the Polish Corps' infantry. Grenadiers wore the same uniform of the musketeers shown here, but with a flaming grenade badge on the front of the headgear and a white decorative feather on the left side of the headgear.

raised in 1792 from Ukrainians who were loyal to the Commonwealth), the Foot Guard Regiment of the Grand Duchy of Lithuania and the 1st Lithuanian Regiment of Advance Guard Lancers. All the Polish-Lithuanian artillery companies and the single corps of pontoniers were absorbed into the Russian military forces. In addition to the units listed above, the Russian Army also absorbed the best military corps that had been raised by the Targowica Confederation: one brigade of medium cavalry, one regiment of lancers and one regiment of light cavalry.

The many Polish-Lithuanian soldiers who entered Russian service were obliged to do so by the circumstances since, from a practical point of view, they were like prisoners of war. They hated the Russians who had just invaded their country and thus, with a few exceptions, they would have never been interested in joining the Russian military forces under normal conditions. Catherine the Great did of her best to integrate the Polish-Lithuanian veterans inside her military forces, since she considered these soldiers as a significant military resource that could be employed in future conflicts fought against the Ottoman Empire in the Balkans.

In May 1793 Empress Catherine decreed that the best elements from the Polish-Lithuanian soldiers in Russian service had to be re-organized as an autonomous "Polish Corps" that would have been part of the Russian Army. This would have consisted of two divisions, the first of which was known as "Ukrainian Division" since it comprised a significant number of former Cossacks.

The 1st Polish Division consisted of two infantry regiments (one of grenadiers and one of musketeers), four cavalry brigades, four Light Horse regiments and seven companies of artillery. The infantry regiments had two battalions each, the cavalry brigades had twelve squadrons each and the Light Horse regiments had eight squadrons each.

Trooper of the Polish Corps' cavalry brigades. This yellow uniform with light blue facings was quite peculiar.

Trooper of the Polish Corps' Light Horse regiments.

The 2nd Polish Division consisted of just two infantry regiments (having two battalions each) and one cavalry brigade. According to the original plans it was to comprise several other units (one infantry regiment, one cavalry brigade, three Light Horse regiments and four companies of artillery) but these all mutinied or fled abroad before the formation of the 2nd Polish Division. The Russians were never happy about their new Polish Corps, since its members were reluctant to serve under a foreign flag and were ready to mutiny at the first occasion; as a result, already on 23 April 1794, Catherine the Great ordered the disbandment of the two Polish divisions and the disarmament of all the Polish-Lithuanian soldiers.

Minor Foreign Contingents

Trooper of the "Yekaterinoslav Hussars", wearing the new uniform used during 1789-1792. Before becoming the mounted bodyguard of Prince Potemkin, the "Yekaterinoslav Hussars" were dressed entirely in light blue. Potemkin loved flamboyant uniforms; during 1790-1792, for example, he issued a very ornate dress to the cuirassier regiment that was tasked with acting as his personal guard ("Prince Potemkin Cuirassiers"). This uniform consisted of a "mitre" cap covered with black fur on the front, red "koller" tunic with black facings and white breeches. On parade a richly-embroidered yellow "soubreveste" was worn over the red "koller" tunic.

In addition to the Greek and Polish-Lithuanian contingents, the Russian Army of Catherine the Great did comprise some other small "foreign corps". On 9 July 1765, from loyal Ossetian mountaineers living in the Caucasus around Mozdok, a "Mozdok Mountaineer Detachment" was formed. This consisted of 200 semi-regular light infantrymen, who were the first mountain troops ever raised by the Russian Army. In 1784, from the Belarusian lands that had been annexed by Russia following the First Partition of Poland, three "banners" of lancers were raised: the Imperial Belarusian Banner, the Mogilev Banner and the Polotsk Banner. Each of the latter had 200 men; the first was recruited from the most important Belarusian aristocrats who had previously served the Polish-Lithuanian Commonwealth.

Also in 1784, there were Crimean Tatars who were willing to serve in the Russian military forces, and thus two "divisions" (i.e. double-squadrons) of light cavalry were raised. The latter were known as "Tauric Tatar Divisions", since Crimea was also known as "Tauride" by the end of the 18th century. According to Empress Catherine's plans, seven "banners" of Belarusians and five "double-squadrons" of Tatars had to be raised in 1784, but this was not possible due to the shortage of available manpower and thus only the units listed above could be effectively formed.

In 1787, while fighting against the Turks, Prince Potemkin raised a hussar regiment from Balkan volunteers who were willing to fight against the Ottomans; this, known as "Yekaterinoslav Hussars", was disbanded in 1789. From some of its best elements two independent squadrons of hussars were formed, which acted as the "private" personal guard of Potemkin until being dissolved in 1792. During the Russo-Turkish War of 1787-1792 Prince Potemkin recruited several short-lived corps of "Arnauts", i.e. Balkan irregulars who fought as light infantrymen. In February 1788 most of these were assembled into two mixed units of infantry and cavalry, which numbered 200 men each. In 1792 a volunteer "Corps of Little-Russian Foot Riflemen" was raised from Ukrainian volunteers, while all the irregular units of "arnauts" were disbanded due to the end of the Russo-Turkish War.

Naval infantry

When Catherine the Great became Empress of Russia in 1762, she found both the navy and the naval infantry in a state of neglect. The marines, in particular, consisted of weak independent detachments serving on the various warships of the Russian Navy. In addition to them, the naval infantry comprised a "Battalion of the Admiralty" tasked with performing garrison duties and a few companies that served on the galleys of the Don Flotilla. Catherine had ambitious political objectives that could be reached only by having a modern and powerful navy capable of operating in the Mediterranean Sea with substantial squadrons; as a result, the new Empress soon created a special commission tasked with reforming the Russian Navy. This commission proposed a new organization for the naval infantry, which was approved by Catherine on 22 March 1764. The Russian marines were now to be structured on four battalions having one grenadier company and six musketeer companies each; the four battalions were assembled together in couples in order to form two "divisions" of marines. In time of war, each of the existing battalions could provide some "extra" companies that were assembled together to form another two "additional" battalions of marines. The new naval infantry units created by Catherine the Great performed extremely well during the Russo-Turkish War of 1768-1774, by conducting several effective amphibious operations. The Empress wanted to have naval supremacy also in the Black Sea and thus retained in service the marine companies that served on the galleys of the Don Flotilla; these consisted of one grenadier company and seven musketeer companies.

In November 1777 the marines were reorganized on eight battalions having one grenadier company and four musketeer companies each. In 1782 the number of musketeer companies in each marine battalion was increased to six. In 1777 Empress Catherine decided to raise two "Battalions of the Admiralty", after having disbanded the original one with the reorganization of 1764. The new battalions were to perform garrison duties in the Baltic bases of the Russian Navy and were to consist of veteran marines who were no longer fit for active service. Each of the two units was to comprise one grenadier company and three musketeer companies. The eight battalions of naval infantry organized in 1777 were assembled into two "divisions" with four battalions each; they were trained to operate in the Baltic but – if needed – they could be sent on other fronts. During the Russo-Swedish War of 1788-1790 the Russian marines suffered from a chronic shortage of men and thus had to be supplemented with the formation of one temporary "reserve battalion" and of two battalions of "bombardiers" (the latter were tasked with serving on the rowing ships of the Baltic Fleet). In 1790, following the end of the hostilities with Sweden, the Russian marines were reorganized on two consolidated regiments having two battalions each. A single battalion mustered one company of grenadiers, four companies of musketeers and an artillery

Musketeer of the Baltic Fleet's marines, wearing the new dark green uniform introduced in 1796. During Catherine the Great's reign, all the units that made up the Russian naval infantry were always dressed like the line infantry. The marines, however, wore white trousers during hot months and had a summer uniform that was designed for use in the Black Sea; this consisted of a simple white waistcoat having red folded collar and round cuffs that was worn together with white loose trousers.

section with four light guns. The two battalions of "bombardiers" and the two Battalions of the Admiralty were retained in service.

On 24 May 1792 the two Marine Regiments and the two Bombardier Battalions were transferred from the jurisdiction of the navy to that of the army. After Russia annexed Crimea, the naval infantry forces operating on the Black Sea were significantly enlarged. The few independent "galley companies", in fact, were expanded in 1785 to become three marine battalions having four musketeer companies each. A single "Company of the Admiralty" was also raised for service in the naval base of Sevastopol. In 1790, by converting some existing foot units of the army, two regiments of "Coastal Grenadiers" were formed for service on the galleys of the Black Sea Fleet of the Russian Navy. These performed very well against the Turks and thus, in

Grenadier of the Baltic Fleet's marines, wearing the new dark green uniform introduced in 1796. This, which was quite similar to that worn by the grenadiers of the Gatchina Troops, comprised Prussian-style "mitre" cap and had red frontal plastron.

Bombardier of the Baltic Fleet, wearing dark green "Potemkin uniform" with black facings. The marines of the Black Sea Fleet were dressed like those of the Baltic Sea Fleet; the "Black Sea Grenadier Corps", instead, was not dressed like the bombardiers of the Baltic Fleet but had a peculiar uniform. This was identical to the Potemkin dress of the line infantry, except for having a dark green squared cap as headgear (identical to that worn by the jager company of the "Izmailovsky" Regiment during 1786-1796).

Gabriele Esposito
Potemkin Uniforms 1786 - 1796

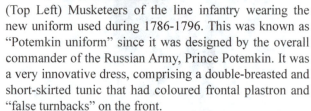

(Top Left) Musketeers of the line infantry wearing the new uniform used during 1786-1796. This was known as "Potemkin uniform" since it was designed by the overall commander of the Russian Army, Prince Potemkin. It was a very innovative dress, comprising a double-breasted and short-skirted tunic that had coloured frontal plastron and "false turnbacks" on the front.

(Top Center) Musicians of the line infantry wearing "Potemkin uniform". The latter comprised as headgear a visored helmet made of leather, having a brass plate on the front and a double-tasselled bag of cloth on the back. The helmet was decorated with a short plume on the left side and with a transverse crest made of fur. For service dress, it was often replaced with a visored round hat, which was red for the line infantry.

(Top Right) Gunner of the artillery sections attached to the line infantry regiments, wearing "Potemkin uniform". As previously, the facing colour of the artillery sections was black. With the new dress introduced in 1786 the grenadiers were dressed exactly like musketeers, except for having a flaming grenade badge on the front of their helmet.

(Bottom Left) Jagers wearing the new "Potemkin uniform" used during 1786-1796.

(Bottom Right) Musician of the jagers, wearing the "Potemkin uniform" used during 1786-1796.

The Russian Army of 1696 - 1796

(Top Left) NCO (left) and trooper (right) of the cuirassiers, wearing the new "Potemkin uniform" used during 1786-1796.

(Top Right) Cuirassier troopers (left) and trumpeters (right), wearing the "Potemkin uniform" used during 1786-1796. Note the profusion of decorative elements embroidered on the dress of the musicians.

(Left) Carabinier trumpeter (left), NCO (centre) and troopers (right) wearing the new "Potemkin uniform" used during 1786-1796.

(Top Left) Dragoon trooper (left) and trumpeter (right), wearing the new "Potemkin uniform" used during 1786-1796. (Top Right) Trooper (left) and trumpeter (right) of the Light Horse regiments, wearing the new "Potemkin uniform" used during 1786-1796. (Bottom Left) Trooper of the Horse Jagers, wearing the "Potemkin uniform" used during 1788-1790. (Bottom Right) Officer (left) and trooper (right) of the Horse Jagers, wearing the uniform used during 1790-1796.

1794, they were reorganized as the "Black Sea Grenadier Corps". This consisted of four battalions with six grenadier companies each. The "naval grenadiers" of the Black Sea Fleet served on rowing ships exactly like the "bombardiers" of the Baltic Sea Fleet; the three marine battalions formed in 1785, instead, served on the "ships of the line" that were operated by the Russians on the Black Sea since 1784. In 1794 the Company of the Admiralty of the Black Sea Fleet was expanded and became a battalion with five companies; at the same time both the "naval grenadiers" and the marines of the Black Sea Fleet were transferred from the jurisdiction of the navy to that of the army. As explained in one of the previous paragraphs, the "Gatchina Troops" of Paul I were initially recruited from the marines of the Baltic Fleet; one unit in particular, the single grenadier battalion, always retained a distinctive "naval infantry" character.

The Cossack Hetmanate of Ukraine

The Cossack Hetmanate

The Ukrainian Cossack state known as "Cossack Hetmanate" was inhabited by the Zaporizhian Cossacks and thus was also known as the "Zaporizhian Host". It emerged as a proper political entity in 1648-1649, after the Zaporizhian Cossacks conducted a successful rebellion against the Polish-Lithuanian Commonwealth. Until that moment, in fact, most of Ukraine's territory had been controlled by the Poles who had fought several wars against the Ottomans and Moscowy to gain possession of the fertile plains. The Turks were strong allies of the Tatars who lived in the Crimean Peninsula; the latter, being located in southern Ukraine and in the northern part of the Black Sea, had a great strategical importance for the Ottoman Empire. By exerting their indirect rule over Crimea, in fact, the Ottomans could control the main commercial routes that crossed the Black Sea and could easily attack Ukraine from the south. The Crimean Tatars, despite their Mongol origins, had converted to Islam and had gradually transformed their state into an Ottoman protectorate; like their famous ancestors they spent most of their lives raiding and pillaging as semi-nomads, earning a living thanks to slave-trading.

Zaporizhian Cossack from the early 18th century, equipped to serve on foot.

The Crimean Tatars attacked Ukrainian lands controlled by Poland-Lithuania on a regular basis in order to capture slaves and booty. The army of the Crimean Khanate primarily consisted of horsemen, still organized according to traditional Mongol models and equipped with old-fashioned weapons. The majority of the Tatar cavalry consisted of mounted archers, having light personal equipment and being armed with deadly composite bows; the Tatar nobles, however, were generally equipped with full armour and thus made up a small corps of heavy cavalry that operated together with the light skirmishers. Military units were formed on a tribal basis: each Tatar noble commanded his own retainers, who were assembled into "banners". More or less the Crimean Khanate could field a total of 25,000 horsemen, who made up the vanguard of the Ottoman Army when the latter operated in Eastern Europe.

To face the serious military problem represented by the Tatars and by their Ottoman allies, during the second half of the 16th century the Poles decided to create some settlements of "farmers-soldiers" on the border that divided their portion of Ukraine from Tatar Crimea. These new settlements had to garrison the defensive line represented by the Dnieper River and thus mostly consisted of small forts, which were inhabited by communities of "freebooters" who gradually transformed themselves into the Zaporizhian Cossacks. Each of the new frontier communities had its own fort or "sich", which controlled a portion of the Ukrainian steppe; all the male inhabitants of one of such fortified camps were required to fight when needed and equipped themselves with firearms in order to contrast in an effective way the raids of the Tatars (who were still equipped with traditional Mongol weapons like the famous composite bow). With the progression of time, several Cossack fortifications built on the Lower Dniepr started to be assembled together in order to form a single stronghold; the latter became the "capital" of the Zaporizhian Cossacks and thus assumed the denomination of "Zaporizhian Sich". Like all the Cossack Hosts existing in Eastern Europe, that of the Zaporizhian Cossacks had a supreme leader known as "Hetman" modelled on the Polish-Lithuanian military hierarchy; the latter had significant political and military powers, but was not an absolute ruler since he was elected by his own community in a democratic way.

In 1572 Sigismund II Augustus of Poland-Lithuania decided to transform the Zaporizhian Cossacks into a permanent component of the Polish-Lithuanian Army, by giving them the new denomination of "Registered Cossacks". The Poles, in fact, had experimented how much the Cossacks could be effective in fighting on the steppes against the Tatars. Not all the Zaporizhian Cossacks, however, were admitted into the ranks of the Registered Cossacks; the latter, in fact, enjoyed a series of privileges in exchange for their military services: they were freemen and not serfs, they were exempted from the payment of taxes and duties, they received wages from the Polish-Lithuanian government and were permitted to own some land. Like it happened in Russia with the Don Cossacks, the free lifestyle of the Cossack communities started to attract thousands of peasants who lived as serfs on the lands of the Polish-Lithuanian Commonwealth and who decided to leave their homes in order to become Cossacks. This caused frequent clashes between the Zaporizhian leaders and the Polish aristocrats who owned most of the Ukrainian lands, especially after the Cossacks started to ask for an expansion of the number of Registered Cossacks.

In 1648, after several minor Cossack rebellions had been crushed with violence by the Poles, the Zaporizhians rose up in revolt under the guidance of the expert Bohdan Khmelnitsky (who was an important commander of the Registered Cossacks). In order to win their freedom from the Polish-Lithuanian Commonwealth, for the first time in their history the Ukrainian Cossacks allied themselves with the Crimean Tatars. Against all odds the uprising was a complete success, despite the fact that both the Russians and the Don Cossacks had decided to side with the Poles during the struggle. During the previous years the Zaporizhian Sich had become a significant regional power of Eastern Europe, capable of launching naval incursions against the very heart of the Ottoman Empire as well as of developing new commercial routes; for this reason, both the Poles and the Russians were strongly determined to cancel the autonomy of the Ukrainian Cossacks. The latter had a strong allegiance to the Orthodox Church and this put them at odds with the Catholic-dominated Polish-Lithuanian Commonwealth; many religious refugees coming from Poland, in fact, joined the Zaporizhian communities in Ukraine.

The Cossack uprising led by Bohdan Khmelnitsky greatly weakened the Polish-Lithuanian Commonwealth and officially came to an end in 1654, with the signing of the Treaty of Pereyaslav. According to the latter the Cossack Hetmanate of the Zaporizhians became fully independent from Poland-Lithuania and was recognized as a proper state. In order to defend their newly acquired freedom, however, the Cossacks accepted to put their nation under the military protection of Russia and thus pledged their loyalty to the Tsar. The Russians had extended their sphere of influence to southern Ukraine by forming an alliance with the Zaporizhian Cossacks, but for the moment they were in no conditions to limit the freedom of the latter.

Contrary to what one might think, the Cossack Hetmanate of Ukraine had a proper "regular" army that included several different kinds of military units. These could be divided into three main categories: "guard" corps that were placed at the direct orders of the Hetman, the "City Army" and the "Lowland Army". At the beginning of the 18th century the personal troops of the Hetman consisted of the following: a small "ceremonial" bodyguard made up of 80 elite soldiers, a certain number of noble "retainers" who served with their own armed servants, a corps of 50 cavalrymen equipped as western-style dragoons, one squadron of Wallachian light cavalry and several companies of "chosen" infantry.

The "City Army" consisted of the former regiments of Registered Cossacks that had been part of the Polish-Lithuanian Army, which continued to exist also after the Zaporizhians became independent. The "City Army" comprised a total of ten regiments that were structured according to the traditional administrative subdivisions of the Hetmanate; these semi-permanent military units were known as "city regiments" because each of them was named after the most important urban centre of each Zaporizhian province: Hadiach, Kiev, Lubny, Myrhorod, Nizhyn, Pereiaslav, Poltava, Pryluky, Starodub and Chernihiv. Each of these cities was the recruiting centre for one regiment, where all the men coming from nearby villages had to gather in order to form their own unit. Generally speaking, each village sent its men already assembled into "sotni" or "hundreds". Each regiment had a different internal establishment and thus mustered a different number of "sotni", which was determined according to the population of its province. The members of the "city regiments" were exempt from paying taxes and from performing labour services, but were obliged to perform military service without pay and had to buy their own personal equipment. All the regiments of the "City Army" were cavalry ones.

The units making up the "Lowland Army" were commonly known as "mercenary regiments", due to the fact that they were recruited by colonels (nominated by the Hetman) from volunteers who wished to serve as professional full-time soldiers. At the beginning of the 18th century, they were six in total, four of infantry and two of cavalry. Being permanent corps - differently from the "city regiments" - they were also employed as police forces by the authorities of the Hetmanate. These units were extremely loyal to the Hetman, who paid and equipped them: for this reason, they were tasked with defending him in case of internal uprisings and garrisoned the most important fortifications of the Hetmanate. All the "mercenary regiments" were organized into "hundreds" and were named after their commanding colonel. Each of them had a different internal establishment and thus mustered a different number of "sotni".

The Cossack Hetmanate of Ukraine, as a state, had a series of peculiarities that made it sensibly different from all the other nations existing in Eastern Europe during the 18th century. Among the Zaporizhians supreme power belonged to the General Cossack Council, which was made up of all the free Cossacks capable of bearing arms; this assembly elected in a democratic way its head, i.e. the Hetman. The latter was supported in performing his important functions by an advising body known as the "Council of Officers"; this included the most important Cossack officers of each regiment making up the "City Army". With the progression of time, however, the General Cossack Council started to loose most of its previous importance since – for example – the new Hetmans started to be chosen by the Council of Officers. The Hetman exerted complete control over the administration, the judiciary, the finances and the military forces of the Zaporizhian Sich. His personal cabinet, which usually included some of his relatives and personal friends, functioned both as the general staff of the Zaporizhian Army and as the cabinet of ministers of the Cossack state. The Hetman was also responsible for addressing the foreign policy of his nation, something that was extremely complex in times of trouble like the beginning of the 18th century.

Noble warlord of the Crimean Tatars from the early 18th century.

Each of the ten regimental/administrative districts in which the territory of the Cossack Hetmanate was divided had a governor, who also acted as the commanding colonel of the regiment that was levied from his district. The regiments of the "City Army" thus represented the core of the Zaporizhian military forces, because they were strongly linked to their home territories and to their communities. With the progression of time, however, the "mercenary" military units placed under the direct control of the Hetman became increasingly important due to the fact that they were made up of professional soldiers. The regiments of the "City Army" had a semi-permanent nature, since they were mobilized only in case of war or to face the incursions of the Crimean Tatars; they were made up of light cavalrymen armed with flintlock weapons, who usually acted as a sort of "mounted infantry" that was capable of moving very rapidly on the Ukrainian plains.

The Zaporizhian Cossacks travelled long distances on horseback but often dismounted to fight, in order to use in a more effective way their firearms. Each colonel was responsible for mobilizing and training the regiment he commanded; originally he was elected by the free Cossacks living in his home district, but with the progression of time Zaporizhian colonels started to be appointed by the ruling Hetman. Each Cossack colonel had a personal military staff consisting of a quartermaster, a judge, a chancellor, an adjutant and a standard-bearer. The social structure of the Cossack Hetmanate comprised five distinct groups: the nobility, the free Cossacks, the clergy, the townspeople and the peasants. The aristocracy consisted of old noble families that had not succumbed to "Polonization" during the previous centuries and of emergent Cossack officers who had come to control large land properties.

The new Zaporizhian nobility emerged after the Ukrainian lands that had belonged to the Polish aristocracy were re-distributed; it did not work according to a hereditary system but its survival was determined by its level of loyalty towards the Hetmanate's new regime. This partly changed with the progression of time, since during the 18th century the lands and privileges of the Cossack officers became hereditary. The Orthodox clergy enjoyed a very high status in the Zaporizhian Sich, since it controlled large land properties that were exempt from the payment of taxes.

Inside the Cossack Hetmanate 12 major cities enjoyed some special self-governing rights; these administered their own courts of justice and financial resources in an autonomous way. The inhabitants of such cities earned a living as merchants or as craftsmen; several of them became enough wealthy to buy titles of nobility. The peasants living on the territory of the Cossack Hetmanate who could not perform as soldiers were all free men, who owned some land. With the progression of time, however, the properties of many peasants were absorbed by the estates of the nobility and thus an increasing number of peasants was forced to work for landlords. Their obligations, in any case, remained much lighter than those of the peasant serfs living in the Polish-Lithuanian Commonwealth or in the Russian Empire. The Ukrainian peasants, for example, were free to move on the territory of the Hetmanate together with their families and goods.

The Cossack Hetmanate extended itself over most of central Ukraine and its lands were crossed by the Dniepr River, which divided them in two parts having more or less the same extension. Following the international recognition of the Zaporizhian Cossacks' independence in 1654, both Poland-Lithuania and Russia nurtured the ambition of destroying the Cossack Hetmanate at the first occasion. The Poles were interested in exerting their influence over the portion of Cossack territories that was located west of the Dniepr River, while the Russians were interested in conquering the portion of Cossack territories that was located east of the Dniepr River; these, despite being part of the same Cossack state, were respectively known as "Right-bank Ukraine" and "Left-bank Ukraine".

When the Great Northern War broke out, the Cossack Hetmanate was guided by the ambitious and capable Ivan Mazepa who, during the first phase of the hostilities, understood that his state could take advantage of the ongoing situation by weakening both Polish-Lithuania and Russia in order to increase its political autonomy. In 1702 Mazepa supported a Cossack revolt that took place in Right-bank Ukraine, taking advantage of Poland-Lithuania's military weakness; six years later, on 28 October 1708, the Zaporizhian Hetman concluded an alliance with Charles XII of Sweden who was invading Russia at the head of a large army. Upon learning of Mazepa's unexpected political move, Peter the Great decided to act very rapidly in order to keep control over Left-Bank Ukraine. He sent Prince Menshikov, the most important commander of the Russian Army, against the Cossack territories at the head of 25,000 men. The latter marched on the capital of the Cossack Hetmanate, which was the city of Baturyn at that time. Despite being a fortified urban centre, Baturyn was stormed by the Russians and most of its inhabitants were massacred. Following this dramatic event, the Zaporizhian Cossacks divided themselves into two groups: one remained loyal to Mazepa and continued the war together with the Swedes, while the other elected a new pro-Russia Hetman (Ivan Skoropadsky). In June 1709, on the territory of the Cossack Hetmanate, the most decisive battle of the Great Northern War was fought at Poltava between the Russians and the Swedes; the clash saw Charles XII being soundly defeated and put an end to Mazepa's dreams of transforming the Cossack Hetmanate into a fully-independent state protected by the Swedish military power. Following the Battle of Poltava, the Zaporizhian Sich's autonomy became only nominal since the Russians started to choose both the Hetmans and the colonels of the various regiments. The military forces of the Cossack state were reduced in a significant way, since all the regiments of the "Lowland Army" were ordered to be disbanded as early as 1709.

In 1722 Peter the Great established the so-called "Little Russian Collegium", i.e. a body of six Russian military officers who were permanently stationed in the Cossack Hetmanate in order to act as a "parallel government". The "Little Russian Collegium" existed for just a few years but transformed the Zaporizhian nation into a Russian puppet state. The Cossack Hetmanate was no longer permitted to conduct its own foreign relations without following Saint Petersburg's indications and could no longer welcome peasant serfs fleeing from the territories of the Russian Empire. The transformation of the Cossack Hetmanate into a Russian protectorate had important consequences for the Zaporizhian military forces, which were significantly weakened in their numbers and combat capabilities.

The "court troops" placed at the direct orders of the Hetman were reorganized as one infantry company and one cavalry squadron. The latter was formed by assembling together the best elements of the ten regiments that made up the "City Army"; its members performed a variety of functions that included escorting the Hetman during his voyages as well as protecting the Council of Officers and delivering official messages written by the Hetman. The elite cavalry squadron started to be made up of volunteers since 1743 and comprised 120 men in 1750; internally it was sub-divided into three sections with 40 men each. The unit also worked as a sort of military academy for those young Zaporizhian aristocrats who wanted to become officers, since attached to its ranks there was a variable number of "cadets" who underwent military training. The official denomination of the Hetman's mounted bodyguard was "Companion Banner". Its members were paid by the central government and were provided with the needed military equipment. In 1752 the "Companion Banner" was re-structured as two autonomous companies, each of which consisted of the following elements: three officers, six NCOs, two drummers and 90 troopers. One company was tasked with following the Hetman during his voyages, while the other garrisoned his residence. While the mounted bodyguard underwent these organizational modifications, the company of foot guardsmen was progressively reduced to a small detachment that was attached to the "Companion Banner".

In 1764 the Russians decided to abolish the figure of the Hetman and thus the two companies making up the latter's personal guard were disbanded; their members were employed to form a new guard corps, consisting of a single infantry company, which was tasked with guarding the most important public buildings of the Zaporizhian state. The new company was trained and dressed according to contemporary Russian models; it was disbanded in 1775 when the Zaporizhian Sich was formally annexed to the Russian Empire. For what regards the evolution of the other military forces deployed by the Cossack Hetmanate, we have already anticipated that the "mercenary" regiments making up the "Lowland Army" were all disbanded by the Russians in 1709. It should be noted, however, that three of such units did not join Hetman Mazepa in his anti-Russian rebellion and thus their members entered Russian service after the disbandment of the "Lowland Army". With these professional Ukrainian soldiers, the Russian authorities organized two Cossack regiments that were tasked with policing the territory of Left-bank Ukraine on their behalf. In 1728 these were increased to three regiments, but continued to have the usual semi-regular nature that was typical of Cossack corps. In 1775, following the disappearance of the Cossack Hetmanate, they were reorganized as three regular light cavalry regiments of the Russian Army. Each of the latter had six squadrons and was named after the city in which it was garrisoned: 1st "Kiev" Light Horse Regiment, 2nd "Siversk" Light Horse Regiment and 3rd "Chernihiv" Light Horse Regiment.

The ten regiments that made up the "City Army" of the Cossack Hetmanate retained their traditional organization until 1764, when the figure of the Hetman was abolished by the Russians. During that year most of them were disbanded and their members were assembled together with the Balkan settlers living on the territory of Ukraine - in the settlements of New Serbia and Slavonic Serbia - to form six new regiments of regular light cavalry. The latter consisted of two hussar regiments, known as "Black Hussars" and "Yellow Hussars", that were mostly recruited from the Balkan communities and of four lancer regiments that were mostly recruited from Zaporizhian Cossacks. Each of the new lancer units consisted of 16 mounted companies and 4 infantry companies; in time of war the former were assembled into 8 squadrons with two companies each, while the latter were to serve as garrison units. In 1776, following the disappearance of the Cossack Hetmanate, the last surviving regiment of the "City Army" was disbanded by the Russians and thus the latter could raise some more units of regular lancers from former Zaporizhian Cossacks. Two new regiments were added to the existing ones, bringing the total of Ukrainian lancer units included into the Russian Army to six. According to the new internal organization introduced in 1776, each regiment of lancers was to consist of six squadrons with two mounted companies each.

In 1783, following the annexation of the Crimean Khanate to Ukraine, the Russians decided to reorganize their regular Ukrainian cavalry units. The three regiments of "Light Horse" that had been "regularized" in 1775 were retained in service but received the new official denomination of "Carabiniers"; the six regiments of lancers, instead, were assembled together in couples to form three new regiments of regular Cossacks. In 1783 another six new regiments of Cossacks were created, by assembling together non-Ukrainian light cavalry units that already existed in the Russian Army: one regiment from the Hungarian Hussars and Moldavian Hussars, one regiment from the Serbian Hussars and Bulgarian Hussars, one regiment from the Illyrian Hussars and Wallachian Hussars, one regiment from the Macedonian Hussars and Dalmatian Hussars and one regiment from a temporary hussar corps made up of former Zaporizhian Cossacks. Each of the new regiments had six squadrons with two companies each. Just a few months after their formation, the new units received the new official denomination of "Carabiniers".

In addition to those described above, the Russian Army of 1762 did comprise also some other units recruited from Ukraine; these were those made up of Slobodian Cossacks and Bakhmut Cossacks. By the time of Catherine the Great's ascendancy to the Russian throne the first were made up of five regiments while the latter consisted of a single weak regiment. In 1756 the best elements coming from the Slobodian Cossack regiments were assembled together in order to form a new hussar corps, the "Slobodian Hussars"; some years later, in 1764, the regiment of Bakhmut Cossacks was transformed into a regular regiment of lancers.

Russian Regimental Flags and Colors

In many European Regiments there was a "White" flag, often called the "Colonel's Color" or "Lieb" Flag and "Colored" flags which are often referred to as the "Regimental Flag". In the early period, the regiment could have several colored flags, one for each battalion – each of a different color. Most of this information comes from R.D. Pengel and G.R. Hunts', *Russian Infantry Uniforms and Flags of the Seven Year's War*.

The basic description of each flag consisted of a brown double-headed eagle. The crowns, beaks, sun rays, scepter, imperial monogram, and orb were gold. The coat of arms in the center was enclosed in gold. The tail of the eagle had the cross of St Andrew surrounded by gold chains. The flames were arranged in the corners creating a "cross" in the center.

For the Russian Corps of Observation, each Regiment had a "white" flag and several colored flags that were 1.42 x 2.13 m.

Ground Color	Flames
White	Gold
Blue	Raspberry
Cherry	White
Green	Raspberry
Light Blue	Yellow
Yellow	Gold

Musketeers of the line regiments had one white and one colored flag. The flags were 1.82 x 2.66 m. The staff was 3.55 m in length and painted red. The White flag had shields on the eagle that had either the city coat-of-arms or the arms of Moscow.

The colored flag had various base flag colors and flame colors. Instead of the eagle, the center had the coat-of-arms of the city or Moscow. All shields were gold except for the Archangelski, Viatski and Iaroslavski regiments, which were silver. This is from the reign of Empress Anne and it was supposedly carried over by subsequent rulers until the changes of 1800.

An example of a "White" (Left) and "Colored" (Right) flags of the Rostov Regiment.

An example of the "Colored" (Left) and "White" (Right) flags of the 3rd Grenadiers.

The Russian Army of 1696 - 1796

Regimental Name	Flag Color	Flame Color
Azov	Red	Yellow
Archangel	Green	Red
Astrakhan	Red	Yellow
Boutyr	Green	Red
Belozersk	Orange	Green
Veliki-Loutzk	Sky Blue	Red
Vladimir	Green	Red
Vologod	Blue	Yellow
Voronezh	Sky Blue	Red
Vyborg	Green	Red
Viataki	Blue	Yellow
Ingermanland	Green	Red
Kazan	Green	Red
Kexholm	Yellow	Red
Kievsky	Red	Yellow
Koporsk	Green	Red
Ladoga	Green	Red
Moskov (1st/2nd)	Blue	Yellow
Mourom	Green	Red
Narva	Sky Blue	Red
Neva	Green	Red
Novgorod	Orange	Green
Nijenovgorod	Sky Blue	Red
Perm	Green	Red
Pskov	Orange	Green
Rostov	Yellow	Red
Riazan	Blue	Yellow
St Petersburg	Green	Red
Sibir	Green	Red
Smolensk	Blue	Yellow
Suzdal	Green	Red
Tobolsk	Green	Red
Troitzk	Green	Red
Ouglitz	Sky Blue	Red
Chernigov	Yellow	Red
Schusselburg	Red	Yellow
Iaroslav	Sky Blue	Red

The guard regiments consisted of the following:

	White Flag	**Colored Flags**	**Borders**
Preobrazhensky	one	seven	Red
Semenovsky	one	five	Sky Blue
Ismailovsky	one	five	Green

The colored flags for all three regiments were orange.

The Regiments of Grenadiers had one white flag with red flames and three red flags with white flames. It measured 1.42 x 3.62 m with a white staff measuring 3.62 in tall. The eagle was the same as above, but the arms of Moscow were around the neck. The eagle was posted on a cloud with banners, cartridge boxes, and miters in it.

Some of the regiments we are aware of are:

Pskov – Sky blue, green cloud, brown panther, hand emerging from the cloud
Rostov – Red, Green ground with white stag with yellow horns and hoofs
Riazan – Yellow, Green ground, princes with red capes, clothes, fur-lined on coats, boots, and hat.
St. Petersburg – Red, A golden scepter with two crossed iron anchors.
Sibir – White, with two sables in black and gold scroll above. A golden crown and two black arrows with red feathers.
Smolensk – White, with green ground. White bird on a black cannon with yellow woodwork.
Suzdal – Upper area blue and lower area red. White falcon with a golden prince's crown on its head.
Tobolsk – Sky blue. Golden pyramid with multi-colored trophies.
Troitzk – Red with a Golden crown and cross.
Ouglitz – Red with a green ground. Young tsarevich Dimitri dressed in complete gold from head to toe. He is holding a knife in one hand and a young sacrificial lamb in the other.
Chernigov – White with a black eagle and a yellow crown, beak, claws, and cross.
Schlusselburg – Blue, with a green ground. White fortress with a gold key and crown.
Iaroslav – Yellow on a green ground. A black bear armed with a red halberd.

Battle honors of Russian Infantry Regiments

Gross-Jagersdorff (19 August 1757)
Palov, Apcheren, Archangel, Boutyr, Belozersk, 1st Grenadiers, Voronezh, Novogrod, Troitzk, Viataki, Nijenovgorod, Chernogov, Muromon, 2nd Grenadiers, St. Petersburg, 2nd Moskov, Schlusselburg, Kiev, Vyborg, Kazan, Narva, Rostov, 3rd Grenadiers, Ladoga, Nevsky, Sibir, Vologod, Azov, Ougiltz and Sudal.

Zorndorf (14 August 1758)
1st Grenadiers, 2nd Grenadiers, 3rd Grenadiers, 4th Grenadiers, Nevsky, Rostov, Chernigov, Troitzki, Schlusselburg, St Petersburg, Novgorod, Voronezh, Riazan, Kazan, Smolenski, Muromon, Butyr, Kexholm, Ladoga, Suzdal, and the 1st, 3rd, 4th and 5th regiments of Musketeers of the Corps of Observation.

Zullichau (12 July 1759)

1st Grenadiers, 4th Grenadiers, Azov, Archangel, Viataki, Bizov, Vyborg, 2nd Moskov, Sibir, Perm, Kiev, 2nd Grenadiers, 3rd Grenadiers, Narva, Rostov, Pakov, Vologod, Belozersk, Nijenovgorod, Voronezh, Novgorod, St. Petersburg, and the Grenadiers, 1st and 5th Regiments of Musketeers.

Kunersdorf (28 August 1759)

1st Grenadiers, 3rd Grenadiers, 4th Grenadiers, Vologod, Neva, Kazan, Azov, Perm, 2nd Moskov, Nizov, Sibir, Viataki, Ouglitz, Kiev, Apcheron, Rostovski, Pakov, Belosersk, Nijenovgorod, 2nd Grenadiers, Novgorod, St Petersburg, Voronezh, Narva, Archangel, Chernogov, Vyborg and the Grenadiers and the 1st, 3rd, 4th and 5th Regiments of Musketeers.

According to Keith Over, the cavalry carried one "white" flag and four "colored" flags by 1797. The Cuirassier standards were rectangular brocade with ciphers in the corners, and embroidery along the edges. On the pole side, bottom was the double-headed eagle in gold with one wing pointing to the opposite corner which would have a device (sunburst or cross). The backgrounds for the corner ciphers were in the regimental color while the laurels, monograms, border fringes, and foliage pattern were all in a metallic color for the individual regiments. The cross was gold while the rays were silver.

For the Dragoons, the flags were square. The central device was a double-headed, black eagle in an orange circle. The corners were colored to form the appearance of a cross on the flag against the base color. The crowns, beak, feet, orb, scepter, and chain were all in gold. The wreath was green.

An example of a Russian Infantry flag from the reign of Paul I

The distinctions for the Cuirassiers were:

Regiment	"Colored" background and corner device	"White" Corner device	Metal
Emperor's Lieb	Light Blue / White	Light Blue	Silver
Empress's Lieb	Deep Pink / Light Blue	Deep Pink	Silver
Military Order	Black / White	Black	Gold
Gloukhov	Beige / Orange	Beige	Silver
Ekaterinoslav	Orange / Light Blue	Light Blue	Silver
Kazan	Green / Red	Red	Gold
Kievsky	Deep Yellow / Purple	Deep Purple	Silver
Malorossii	Purple / Light Green	Purple	Gold
Nejin	Red / White	White	Gold
Rejin	Beige / Light Blue	Light Blue	Gold
Riazan	Light Blue / White	Light Blue	Gold
Sofii	Orange / Light Blue	Light Blue	Gold
Starodoubov	Dark Green / White	Dark Green	Silver
Kharkhov	Pink / Puce	Puce	Silver
Chernogov	Yellow / Puce	Puce	Silver
Iambourg	Green / White	Green	Gold
Neplouieva	Deep Pink / Dark Grey	Dark Grey	Silver
Frideritsia	Mauve / Orange	Mauve	Gold
Zorna	Yellow / Red	Yellow	Gold

The Russian Army of 1696 - 1796

The distinctions for the Dragoons were:

Regiment	"Colored" background and corners	"White" Corners	Metal
Astrakhan	Yellow / Lt. Blue	half Lt. Blue / half Yellow	Silver
Hastatova	half red / half white Dark blue	half red / half dark blue	Silver
Ingermanland	Deep Pink / White	Deep Pink	Gold
Irkutsk	Lt Blue / Red	half Red / half Lt. Blue	Gold
Kargopol	Lt. Blue / White	Lt. Blue	Silver
Moskov	Orange / Lt. Blue	half Orange / half Lt. Blue	Silver
Narva	Purple / White	Purple	Silver
Nijenovgorod	half Lt. Orange Half White, Black	half Lt. Orange / Black	Silver
Orenburg	Red / White	Red	Gold
Pskov	Yellow / White	Yellow	Gold
Rostov	Blue / White	Blue	Silver
Sversk	Orange / Black	half Black / half Orange	Silver
Shreidersa	half White / half Dark Green. White	White / half Dark Green	Gold
Sibir	Red / Green	half red / half Green	Silver
Smolensk	Orange / Purple	half Orange / half Purple	Gold
St. Peterburg	Green / White	Green	Gold
Taganroga	Red / Yellow	half Yellow / half Red	Gold

Bibliography

Dotsenko, V.D., *The Russian Naval Uniform 1696-1917*, Logos, 1994

Esposito, G., *Armies of the Great Northern War 1700-1720*, Osprey Publishing, 2019

Friedrich, W., *Die Uniformen der Kurfurstlich Sachsischen Armee 1683-1763*, Arbeitskreises Sachsischen Militärgeschichte, 1998

Haythornthwaite, P., *The Russian Army of the Napoleonic Wars (I)*, Osprey Publishing, 1987

Haythornthwaite, P., *The Russian Army of the Napoleonic Wars (II)*, Osprey Publishing, 1987

Kling, S., *Sweden's Cossack allies during the Great Northern War*, in "Great Northern War Compendium" vol.I, THGC Publishing, 2015

Kling, S., *The Army of Holstein-Gottorp in the Great Northern War*, in "Great Northern War Compendium" vol.I, THGC Publishing, 2015

Kling, S., *The Emergence of the Russian Army*, in "Great Northern War Compendium" vol.II, THGC Publishing, 2015

Konstam, A., *Russian Army of the Seven Years' War (I)*, Osprey Publishing, 1996

Konstam, A., *Russian Army of the Seven Years' War (II)*, Osprey Publishing, 1996

Kuhn, A., *The military forces of the Duchies of Schlesswig-Holstein-Gottorp and the military states of the Upper Saxon Circle*, Editions Brokaw, 1991

Letin, S., *Russian Imperial Guards*, Slavia, 2005

Mollo, B., *Uniforms of the Imperial Russian Army*, Blandford Books, 1987

Nafziger, George F. & Worley, Warren, *The Imperial Russian Army (1763 - 1815) Vol I*, The Nafziger Collection, 1996.

Nafziger, George F. & Worley, Warren, *The Imperial Russian Army (1763 - 1815) Vol II*, The Nafziger Collection, 1996.

Over, Keith, *Flags and Standards of the Napoleonic Wars*, Bivouac Books, 1976

Pappas, N.C., *Greeks in Russian military service in the late 18th and early 19th century*, Institute for Balkan Studies, 1991

Paradowski, M., *The once glorious and powerful Polish-Lithuanian Commonwealth Army*, in "Great Northern War Compendium" vol.I, THGC Publishing, 2015

Pengel, R. D. & Hunt, G.R., *Russian Infantry Uniforms and Flags of the Seven Years War*, On Military Matters, 2004

Querengasser, A., *Die Armee Augusts des Starken im Nordischen Krieg*, Zeughaus Verlag GmbH, 2013

Rospond, V., *Polish Armies of the Partitions 1770-1794*, Osprey Publishing, 2013

Rospond, V., *Polish-Lithuanian Regiments 1717-1794*, Winged Hussar Publishing, 2022

Shamenkov, S., *The Man of War*, Tempora, 2021

Shamenkov, S., *Ukrainian Cossack forces in the Great Northern War*, in "Great Northern War Compendium" vol.II, THGC Publishing, 2015

Index

A
active companies, 34
Admiralty, battalion of the, 28, 93
Advance Guard Regiment, 90
Albanian Battalions, 89–90
Anna, 19, 44
Army of Holstein-Gottorp, 111
artillery, 2, 15, 17, 28–30, 41–43, 51, 53–54, 62, 82
Artillery and Technical Corps, 82
Artillery Battalion, 45–46, 51
artillery detachments, 32, 48, 53, 62
Artilleryman of Moscow's Legion, 65
artillery sections, 20–21, 29–30, 32–33, 41, 54, 61–63, 82, 94–95
Astrakhan Cossacks, 39–40
Astrakhan Host, 80
Augustus II, 4–5, 12
Austrian Army, 15–16, 26, 36
Austrian Empire, 15, 26–27, 36
Austrian light infantrymen, 36
Austrian Succession, 25–26, 36
Azov Cossacks, 39

B
Bakhmut Cossacks, 39, 104
Bakhmut Hussars, 76
Balaklava Infantry Battalion, 90
Balaklava Infantry Regiment, 90
Balkan communities, 76, 104
Balkan Light Infantrymen, 36
Balkan light infantrymen in Austrian service, 37
Balkan light troops in Habsburg service, 38
Balkan military settlers, 34, 72
Balkans, 16, 26–27, 34, 36, 72, 88, 91
Baltic Fleet, 93–94, 98
Baltic Sea, 7, 29, 44, 89
Baltic Sea Fleet, 94, 98
Bashkirs, 9, 24, 40, 80–81
battalion of grenadiers, 45–46, 48, 59, 62
battalion of the senate, 85–86
Belarussian Hussars, 76
Black Hussars, 76, 104
Black Hussars and Yellow Hussars, 74
Black Sea, 90, 93–94, 98–99
Black Sea Cossack Host, 80
Black Sea Cossacks, 80
Black Sea Fleet, 94, 98
Black Sea Grenadier Corps, 94, 98
Bombardier Battalions, 48, 53, 94
  independent, 82
Bombardier Company, 11, 17, 30, 41, 48, 53–54
Bombardier Corps, 42
Bombardier Regiment, 82
bombardiers, 11, 15, 17, 32, 41–42, 83, 93–94, 98
Border Garrison Battalions, 85
Boutyrsk Regiment, 8, 12
Bug Cossacks, 80
Bulgarian Hussars, 34, 72, 76, 78, 104

C
Cadet Corps of Foreign Co-religionists, 90
carabiniers, 59, 62, 69–71, 78, 104
Catherine, 1–2, 20, 44, 52–54, 62, 66, 69–70, 80, 82, 85, 88, 90–93
Cavalier-Guards, 14, 20, 24, 30, 46, 52–53, 56
cavalry, 13–14, 17, 24–26, 34–36, 54, 62, 66, 72, 92, 101, 108
cavalry units, regular Ukrainian, 78, 104
Charles XII, 5, 12, 44–45, 102–3
Chernihiv Light Horse Regiment, 76–77, 104
Chuguev Cossacks, 39, 53, 80
Chuguev Fortress, 39
City Army, 76, 100–104
colored flags, 105, 107–8
Companion Banner, 77–78, 103
Corps of Little-Russian Foot Riflemen, 93
Cossack communities, 9, 13, 28, 39, 80, 100
Cossack corps, 53, 103
Cossack Hetmanate, 5–6, 39, 76, 99–104
Cossack Hetmanate of Ukraine, 38, 99–101
Cossack officer of Saint Petersburg's Legion, 67
Cossack regiments, 9, 38, 78, 80, 103–4
Cossacks, 2, 6, 8–9, 13, 15, 27–28, 39–41, 53, 59, 78, 80, 100, 104
  Don, 15, 32, 38–40, 53, 59–60, 79, 100
Cossacks and Irregular Cavalry, 27, 38
Cossacks of Ukraine, 6
Cossack state, 101–3
Cossack units, 40, 79, 91
Cossack uprising, 38, 100

Count Shuvalov, 41
Crimean Khanate, 6, 78, 88, 99, 104
Crimean Tatars, 9, 22, 27, 39, 92, 99–102
cuirassier regiments, 25, 32–33, 45–46, 50, 59, 69–70, 92
cuirassiers, 24–25, 32–33, 46, 48, 58–59, 68–70, 72, 96, 109

D
Dalmatian Hussars, 76, 78, 104
Denmark, 4–6, 44–45
Don Cossack Host, 38
dragoon regiments, 10, 13–15, 23–25, 33, 41, 45–46, 59, 62, 69–70
dragoons, 10, 13–15, 23–25, 32–33, 45–46, 58–59, 62, 68–70, 72, 108, 110
Duchy of Holstein-Gottorp, 6, 44–45
Duchy of Prussia, 5
Duke of Holstein-Gottorp, 5, 44–45

E
elite Preobrazhensky Regiment, 20
Elizabeth, 30, 44
Empress Anna, 1, 19–20, 22, 25
Empress Catherine, 2, 53, 56, 70, 82, 88, 91, 93
Empress Elizabeth, 1, 30–31, 34, 36, 44, 46, 52, 69
Engineer Corps, 43, 84–85
Engineer Regiment, 43
Essen Grenadier Battalion, 47
European armies, contemporary, 31, 41–42, 62

F
field artillery, 17, 28, 32, 41, 83–84
First Moscow Regiment, 8, 12
Flotilla, Don, 29, 93
Foot Guards, 45
Foot Guards regiment, 45, 91
foreign corps, 2, 92
former Zaporizhian Cossacks, 69, 76–78, 80, 104
Frederick, 5, 24, 26, 32, 36, 38, 42, 44–45, 54, 59, 82
  Charles, 44
Frei Corps, 36, 38
Fusilier Regiments, 42–43, 82

G
Gatchina Troops, 53, 58–60, 94, 98

General Cossack Council, 101
General's Dragoon Company, 14
Georgian Hussars, 26–27, 72–74, 76
Georgian Hussars and trooper, 26
German Duchy of Holstein-Gottorp, 44
German states, 4–5
Great Northern War, 2, 4–6, 8, 10, 17, 20, 22, 44–45, 76, 102–3, 111–12
Great Northern War Compendium, 111
Great Northern War Compendium vol.II, 111–12
Greben Cossacks, 38–39
Greek Infantry Regiment, 88–90
Greeks, 88–89
Grenadier Nowograd Garrison, 35
grenadiers, 10–13, 18–19, 21–22, 29–31, 35–36, 45–49, 55, 58–59, 61–64, 66, 87–88, 91, 94–95, 105, 107–8
  naval, 98
Grenadiers of Moscow's Legion, 67
guard corps, 100, 103
guard infantry, 10, 34
guard regiments, 11, 107

H
Habsburgs, 15–16, 26
heavy cavalry, 2, 7–8, 24–25, 59, 62, 99
Hetman, 6, 100–101, 103–4
Holstein, 25, 33, 48–49, 53, 68
Holstein Army, 1, 44–47, 49
Holstein-Gottorp, 5–6, 44–45, 111
Holstein military forces, 46, 52
Holstein military units, 52–53
horse grenadiers, 14, 22, 24–25, 33, 46, 69–70
Horse Jagers, 97
Horse Jägers, 78, 80
Hungarian Hussars, 15, 26–27, 72, 74, 76
Hungarian Hussars and Moldavian Hussars, 78, 104
Hungary, 15–16, 26
hussar corps, temporary, 78, 104
hussars, 15–16, 26–27, 34, 45, 53, 59–60, 72, 74, 76, 78, 80
Hussars of New Serbia, 34, 72

I
Illyrian Hussars, 76, 78, 104
Imperial Guard, 10–11, 13, 15, 17, 19–20, 24–25, 30,

45–46, 48, 52–56, 59
  elite, 14, 59
Imperial Russian Army, 111
infantry, foreign, 7–8
infantry regiments, 12–13, 17, 22, 24–25, 28, 30, 41–43, 45, 48, 54, 91–92
infantry units, naval, 17, 93
Inner Garrison Infantry, 20
Izmailovsky Regiment, 12, 19, 30, 46, 48, 52–55, 59, 94

J
Jäger Corps, 54, 66
jagers, 58, 62, 64, 66–67, 95
Jägers, 38, 54, 59, 66
  company of, 54, 59, 62
  small detachment of, 62, 66

K
Kalmyk light horseman, 37, 79
Kalmyks, 22, 24, 40
Kazan, 38, 40, 107–8
Kettenburg Musketeer Regiment, 47
Khopyor Cossacks, 39
Kiev, 8, 27, 76–77, 101, 104, 107–8
Kingdom of Denmark, 44–45
Kling, 111
Kruger Garrison Regiment, 49

L
Left-Bank Ukraine, 102–3
Life-Company, 30, 34, 46, 52
Life-Cossacks Squadron, 57
Life-Cuirassiers, 46, 48
Life-Cuirassiers Regiment, 48
Life-Dragoons Regiment, 48, 50
Life Guard Cavalry Regiment, 15, 30
Life Guards Artillery Battalion, 54, 59
Life-Guards Artillery Battalion, 60
Life Guards Horse Regiment, 53, 59
Life-Guards Horse Regiment, 30, 54, 56
Life Guards Jager Battalion, 59
Life-Guards Jager Battalion, 54, 58
Life-Hussars, 46, 54, 59
Life Hussar Squadron, 53
Life-Hussars Regiment, 51

Life-Hussars Squadron, 56–57
Life-Regiment, 30
Light Field Detachments, 62
Light Horse Regiment, 69, 76–78, 80, 104
Lithuania, 2, 4–5, 27, 91
Lithuanian Regiment of Advance Guard Lancers, 91
Little Russian Collegium, 103
Lotcova Cuirassier Regiment, 48
Lowland Army, 77, 100–101, 103

M
Macedonian Hussars, 34, 72, 76
Macedonian Hussars and Dalmatian Hussars, 78, 104
Manteuffel Musketeer Regiment, 47
Mediterranean Sea, 88–89, 93
Moldavian Hussars, 26–27, 72, 76, 78, 104
Mongols, 6
Moscow, 4, 7–9, 19–20, 22, 62, 67, 80, 85, 88, 105, 107
Moscow's Legion, 62, 65, 67, 76
Moskov, 107–8
Municipal Streltsy, 7–8
musketeers, 19–22, 29, 31, 34–35, 45–49, 55, 58–59, 62, 64, 66–67, 85–88, 90–91, 93–95, 105, 107–8

N
naval forces, 28–29, 89
New Serbia, 34, 36, 72, 76
  district of, 34, 72
New Serbia and Slavonic Serbia, 34, 72, 76, 104
New Serbians, 34, 72
Nijenovgorod, 107–8
Novgorod, 8, 107–8

O
Oranienbaum, 52–53
Orenburg Cossacks, 39–40
Orenburg Host, 80
Orthodox Christians, 27, 34, 72, 88–89
Ostsee Garrison Infantry, 20, 22
Ottoman Army, 27, 99
Ottoman Empire, 2, 6, 15–16, 27, 88, 91, 99–100
Ottomans, 6, 15–16, 27, 29, 38–40, 80, 88–90, 92, 99

P
Pandur Regiment, 34, 37

Pandurs, 36–37
Paul, 54, 59
Peter, 1–2, 6–17, 19–31, 38–39, 41, 43–46, 52, 54, 85, 102–3
Peter III, 1, 44–46, 48, 52–53
Poland, 2, 4–5, 12, 27, 90, 92, 100
Poland-Lithuania, 2, 4, 6, 99–100, 102
Polish-Lithuanian Army, 2, 100
Polish-Lithuanian Commonwealth, 2, 5, 39, 90, 92, 99–100, 102
Polish-Lithuanian soldiers, 91–92
Pontoon Company, 43
Potemkin, Prince, 70, 80, 92, 95
Potemkin uniform, 83–85, 95–97
Poteshnyi, 9, 11
Preobrazhenskoe, 9, 11–13
Preobrazhenskoe Regiment, 11–13, 30, 54–55
Preobrazhensky Regiment, 17, 19, 30, 48, 53–54, 59
Preradovich Hussars, 34, 72, 76
Prince August Musketeer Regiment, 47, 49
Prince George Ludwig Dragoon Regiment, 48, 50
Prince Potemkin Cuirassiers, 70, 92
Prince William Musketeer Regiment, 47
Prussia, 5, 24, 44–45, 54, 82
Prussian Army, 5, 20, 32
Prussian cuirassiers and dragoons, 33, 69

R

Registered Cossacks, 100
Right-bank Ukraine, 102
River, Don, 29, 38
Rostov, 107–8
Russia, 1–2, 4, 6–9, 11–13, 17, 19–20, 26–29, 36–40, 44–46, 52–53, 62, 89–90, 92–94, 100, 102
Russian Army, 1–2, 7–8, 12, 14, 16–17, 19–20, 23–28, 30, 32–34, 38–46, 52–54, 58–59, 69–70, 72, 76, 80, 85, 90–92, 104, 111
Russian Empire, 8–9, 27, 40, 43–44, 53, 80, 82, 85, 88–89, 102–3
Russian Imperial Guard, 19–20, 30, 48, 52–54, 111
Russian Navy, 17, 28–29, 43, 52, 88–90, 93–94
Russian Regimental Flags, 1, 105
Russo-Turkish War, 88–90, 92–93

S

Saint Petersburg, 4, 15, 19, 22, 25, 52, 62, 64, 80, 85, 87–88
Saint Petersburg's Legion, 62, 64, 67, 76
Samara Hussars, 76
secret howitzer, 41–42
Secret Howitzer Corps, 42
Semyonovskoe Regiment, 11–12, 54–55
Semyonovsky Regiment, 17, 19, 48, 52–53, 59
Serbian communities, 34, 72
Serbian Hussars, 26–27, 72–73, 76
Serbian Hussars and Bulgarian Hussars, 78, 104
Serbian military settlers, 34, 72
Shevich Hussars, 34, 72
Siberia, 28, 33, 38, 40, 62, 80
Siberian Cossacks, 39–40
Siberian Jägers, battalions of, 66
Siversk Light Horse Regiment, 76–77, 104
Slavonian hussars, 34, 72
Slavonic Serbia, 34, 72, 76, 104
Slobodian Cossacks, 39, 104
Slobodian Hussars, 34, 72–73, 76, 104
St Petersburg, 107–8
Streltsy, 7–8
Sweden, 2, 4–6, 29, 44–45, 80, 93, 102
Swedes, 4–7, 12, 70, 80, 89, 103
Swedish Empire, 2, 4, 6

T

Tatar Crimea, 34, 36, 72, 99
Tatars, 6, 39–40, 92, 99–100
technical corps, 41, 43, 82
Terek Cossacks, 39–40, 80
Terek River, 39–40
Trans-Kama Land Militia, 24, 62
Trinity Company, 87–88
Tsar Ivan, 7, 38, 40
Tsar Paul I, 54, 58, 70, 90
Tsar Peter, 2, 16, 26
Tsar Peter II, 19
Tsar Peter III, 44, 54
Turks, 6, 15–16, 27, 88–89, 92, 94, 99

U

Ukraine, 1–2, 6, 9, 13, 22, 38–39, 69–70, 76, 78, 80, 89, 99–101, 104
Ukraine Land Militia, 62–63, 77
Ukrainian Cossacks, 5, 22, 27–28, 39, 76, 100

former, 74–75
Ukrainian Hussars, 76
Ukrainian lancer units, 76, 104
Ukrainian Land Militia, 13, 19, 22, 62
Ukrainian lands, 100, 102
Ukrainian Light Horse, 77
Ukrainian trooper, 77–78
Ukrainian trumpeter, 77–78

V
Volga Cossacks, 38, 40, 80
Volga River, 38, 40
Voronezh, 107–8
Voronez Hussar Regiment, 75

W
Wallachian Hussars, 76, 78, 104
Wallachian light cavalry, 100
Weiss Grenadier Battalion, 47, 49
Winged Hussar Publishing, 112, 114

Y
Yaik Cossacks, 38–39
Yekaterinoslav Host, 80
Yekaterinoslav Hussars, 92
Yellow Hussars, 34, 72, 74, 76, 104

Z
Zaporizhian Army, 2, 76, 101
Zaporizhian Cossacks, 28, 76, 78, 99–100, 102–4
Zaporizhian Hetman, 77, 102
Zaporizhian Host, 5, 78, 99
Zaporizhian military forces, 101, 103
Zaporizhians, 76, 100–103
Zobeltis Hussar Regiment, 51

Look for more books from Winged Hussar Publishing, LLC – E-books, paperbacks and Limited-Edition hardcovers. The best in history, science fiction and fantasy at:
https://www. wingedhussarpublishing.com
https://www.whpsupplyroom.com
or follow us on Facebook at:
Winged Hussar Publishing LLC
Or on twitter at:
WingHusPubLLC
For information and upcoming publications

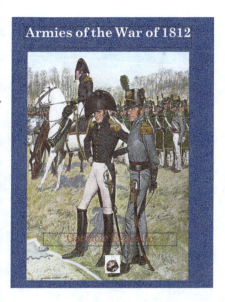
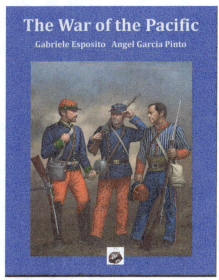
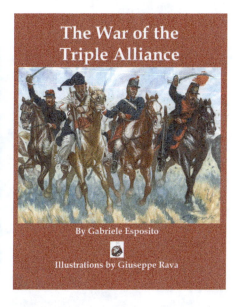
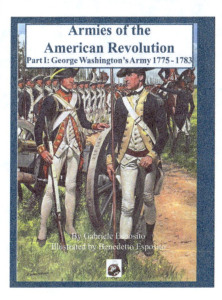
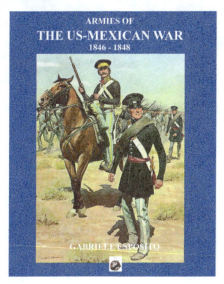
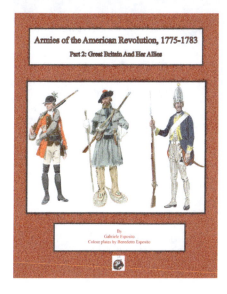